"As the Enneagram has moved from the margins to the mainstream, it's been both used and abused. Many of us know just enough to be dangerous! AJ's recent work is hands down the best resource I know of for the Enneagram and spiritual formation. If the Enneagram is a map for the spiritual journey for different personality types, AJ is a wise, joyful guide for the road. No one should read this book who does not want to change; and anyone who has a deep ache for transformation in the way of Jesus should read this book."

—**John Mark Comer**, pastor of teaching and vision at Bridgetown Church; author of *The Ruthless Elimination of Hurry*

"AJ Sherrill beautifully rescues the Enneagram from the twin mistakes of either elevating it to the be-all, end-all of self-knowledge or reducing it to a parlor game. Through *The Enneagram for Spiritual Formation*, AJ helps us see the Enneagram as a powerful tool in the work of following Christ and being formed into his likeness. Pulling from Scripture, church history, culture, and wisdom from every corner, AJ brings fierce intelligence and profoundly helpful language to this entire conversation. And more than mere ideas, he offers a set of concrete practices for each type to help us flesh out the invitation in our lives, relationships, bodies, and whole selves."

—**Aaron Niequist**, liturgist; author of *The Eternal Current*

"AJ Sherrill has done it! Finally, a way to resource the Enneagram for meaningful discipleship. Through sound wisdom and regular invitations to reflection and practice, AJ calls readers to examine the fullness of who God created them to be and go deeper in life with Christ. Working alongside AJ, I've seen how he lives out these invitations in real time: in his church leadership, his personal relationships, and his own spiritual formation. He knows a valuable truth and has graciously shared it with all of us: No matter our God-given uniqueness, greater transformation and deeper life in Christ are possible. For that reason, this book is a

live."

and, formation and preaching pastor, Bible Church; author of *Human(Kind)*

"So much of what we learn from the Enneagram about ourselves and the people we love stops at simple self-awareness, which can easily become another exercise in self-centered navel-gazing. Thankfully, AJ Sherrill deepens and expands our endeavors, revealing how we can use the wisdom of the Enneagram to draw us closer to the heart of God. Having AJ equip our pastors and staff with the lessons and tools found here in *The Enneagram for Spiritual Formation* developed us in immediate and powerful ways. It will do the same for you."

—**Sean Palmer**, pastor and speaking coach; author of *Forty Days on Being a Three* (Enneagram Daily Reflections) and *Unarmed Empire: In Search of Beloved Community*

"The popularity of the Enneagram has spawned both critics and fanatics in the church. AJ Sherrill artfully connects the Enneagram typology with Scripture, theology, and Christian discipleship. This essential resource will help readers appreciate how personality shapes their faith journey."

—**Mark Scandrette**, adjunct professor, Fuller Theological Seminary; author of *Practicing the Way of Jesus*

"I am deeply grateful for AJ's thoughtful leadership and commitment to forming people in the way of Jesus. He brings the full strength of his thinking around discipleship and spiritual formation to bear on the Enneagram, moving it from a mere construct to discipleship resource. I recommend this book as a helpful and practical tool in this discussion."

—**Jon Tyson**, lead pastor of Church of the City New York; author of *Beautiful Resistance*

"There are a number of books on the Enneagram, many of which never really go deep enough to address spiritual formation. I am thankful to finally have one that moves beyond superficiality and calls Christians to personal transformation. This book is a well of wisdom that shows us how knowing ourselves can in fact make us more like Jesus. I highly recommend it to all who are looking for a Christ-centered introduction to the Enneagram that will help deepen their faith."

—**Winfield Bevins**, author of *Ever Ancient, Ever New*

the enneagram for spiritual formation

How Knowing Ourselves Can
Make Us More Like Jesus

aj sherrill

Brazos Press
a division of Baker Publishing Group
Grand Rapids, Michigan

Published by Brazos Press
a division of Baker Publishing Group
PO Box 6287, Grand Rapids, MI 49516-6287
www.brazospress.com

Printed in the United States of America

Library of Congress Cataloging-in-Publication Data
Names: Sherrill, Andrew (Andrew Jeremy), author.
Title: The enneagram for spiritual formation : how knowing ourselves can make us more like Jesus / A. J. Sherrill.
Description: Grand Rapids, Michigan : Brazos Press, a division of Baker Publishing Group, 2020. | Includes bibliographical references.
Identifiers: LCCN 2020011045 | ISBN 9781587434723 (paperback) | ISBN 9781587435126 (hardcover)
Subjects: LCSH: Typology (Psychology)—Religious aspects—Christianity. | Enneagram. | Jesus Christ—Example. | Christian life.
Classification: LCC BV4597.57 .S54 2020 | DDC 248.401/9—dc23
LC record available at https://lccn.loc.gov/2020011045

Author is represented by the Christopher Ferebee Agency, www .christopherferebee.com.

20 21 22 23 24 25 26   7 6 5 4 3 2 1

In keeping with biblical principles of creation stewardship, Baker Publishing Group advocates the responsible use of our natural resources. As a member of the Green Press Initiative, our company uses recycled paper when possible. The text paper of this book is composed in part of post-consumer waste.

For those disciples who refuse to settle
for a superficial faith

contents

*I*n Christ, you are the beloved.

I believe this is what AJ Sherrill wants you to know, to feel, to experience, to believe in the depths of your soul. And he offers the unique typing system of the Enneagram as a helpful tool to discover your deepest identity.

Now, as AJ will make clear, you are not your Enneatype no more than you—at your core—are a butcher, a baker, or a candlestick maker. Your job title doesn't define you. Your DSM-5 mood disorder doesn't define you. Your gender doesn't even define you. No, you are a beloved image-bearer, in whom God delights.

But there are particular descriptors and diagnoses that help us recognize personality patterns and proclivities that cloud our sense of identity as God's beloved. Our personalities develop in the crucible of early childhood experiences, and we learn to cope—often in painfully unproductive ways—in a broken world. AJ offers the Enneagram as a diagnostic tool to excavate a bit of our inner clutter. He helpfully reminds his readers that "the Enneagram is not a New Age tool. Nor is the Enneagram a 'Christian' tool. The Enneagram is a *human* tool." Because of this, it is a universal tool that helps us grow up.

I appreciate this book for its single-minded simplicity. AJ wants you to grow, to mature, and to discover practices that foster that work. The Enneagram is a tool that aids in a kind of archaeological dig of the soul. Dutch Jew Etty Hillesum, whose precious life was cut short at twenty-nine in the extermination camps of Auschwitz, relentlessly pursued a life of (becoming!) the beloved until her last breath. Shortly before she died, she wrote, "There is a really deep well inside me. And in it dwells God. Sometimes I am there, too. But more often stones and grit block the well, and God is buried beneath. Then He must be dug out again."[1] Her courage in the face of unspeakable evil inspires me to the work.

AJ gives us tools to excavate, to dig through the stones and grit that cover our profound beauty. He offers natural downstream practices for each type alongside challenging upstream practices. He isn't afraid to name our resistance to the life of belovedness, identifying core obstacles for each type. But he also gives us a practice-based pathway to fulfilling our higher aims. If the reader follows the path he paves, she'll identify practices and habits which cultivate flourishing and joy. A significant contribution is a guided "rule of life" that each reader is invited to complete as she navigates the road back home to God, to a life of belovedness.

Why this Enneagram book when there seem to be so many choices? AJ didn't want to replicate other books, but longed to offer the world a discipleship pathway for anyone hungry and thirsty for life, for joy, for rest in an identity that can't be manufactured or achieved. He longs for you to know that you are God's beloved. I'd invite you to take him up on his offer. In these pages, you might just find the reliable road map you need. I am so grateful he wrote it.

When was the last time you were thoroughly captivated, caught up in a moment that you would later reflect on and come to realize had forever altered the course of your life?

I will never forget a moment like that in the spring of 2013. While uttering the four-syllable word, he simultaneously bent down to pet his aged black lab, Venus. *Wait, go back,* I silently thought. Vocabulary was my favorite section on the GRE, but I had never heard this word before. Too embarrassed to raise my hand, I had no clue what the word that had just tumbled from his mouth meant. Leaning over to my friend Mark, I asked, "Did he say *pentagram?*" "No," Mark said. "Father Rohr said *Enneagram.*"

That's what I thought I heard, but this subject matter was foreign territory within my thirty-three-year-old cranium.

Let's back up. Mark Scandrette and I were spending the week studying in the home of Father Richard Rohr, a Franciscan monk and author. Father Rohr was testing out his latest material for the school he was creating, and we were eager learners, sitting at his feet alongside his dog, Venus. For the next hour Father Rohr gushed effortlessly about Enneagram theory. I was captivated. His understanding of psychology (specifically, personality) was incredibly helpful. Little did I know how significantly that hour would alter the course of my studies.

The Gift of Self-Knowledge

The word "Enneagram" means "nine diagram" in Greek. It is a personality theory composed of nine different types. Some refer to the theory as the "faces of the soul."[1] The real gift of this personality theory is self-knowledge. Self-knowledge is the gateway to almost all life change. Although not salvific, self-knowledge is immensely helpful as we endeavor toward transformative growth. As Rohr and Andreas Ebert write in *The Enneagram: A Christian Perspective*, "The gift that the Enneagram gives is self-knowledge or self-awareness. With self-knowledge, the individual can move into pursuing inner-work, which is often painful."[2] The New Testament Epistles are largely concerned with the need for ongoing maturity, for a journey of transformation. One of the best tools in the twenty-first century for Christians who take this journey seriously is the Enneagram. The Enneagram is a theory that yields self-awareness by providing a window into one's self, a means of peering into one's motivations and fears. With this critical self-understanding, one can then orient daily practices and regular rhythms with the possibility of transformation into Christlikeness.

The origins of the Enneagram are disputed. No one knows precisely when and where it originated. (And if they say they do, don't believe them.) The personality theory we have today has developed over centuries and within many cultures. Some connect it with the ancient Sufis, while others look to the desert monks of early Christianity as its forebears. (See the appendix for more on its origins.) Those who may be skeptical of the Enneagram would do well to consider: many of the core themes that today undergird the Enneagram were themes the desert fathers found useful, so we should be careful not to hastily discredit the theory before first examining its fruit.

Episcopal preacher-theologian Fleming Rutledge once quipped to me, "The Enneagram is astrology for Episcopalians." Her point, I think, was that we have missed the plot when we prioritize the Enneagram as central for Christian living. Point taken; the Enneagram is helpful, but it is not essential to human flourishing.

Many, however, do find it helpful. For this reason, it's important to be aware of two groups who dismiss the Enneagram for different reasons.

First, progressive cynics (the early adopters): they mock the Enneagram because it recently entered the evangelical mainstream. To these cynics, I say: Consider the possibility that you are suffering from chronological snobbery and that the Enneagram you despise today was the same tool you held as sacred just a short time ago.

Second, those who dismiss the tool out of fear or ignorance: they often conflate the Enneagram with New Age enlightenment (or something like that). This group of despisers—oftentimes conservative Christians—gives way too much credit to a tool that is merely meant to exist as a filter to help us become more self-aware. The Enneagram is not a New Age tool. Nor is the Enneagram a "Christian" tool. The Enneagram is a *human* tool. Think of the Enneagram like we think of money. Money is a tool. It is neither evil nor good. Money is neutral. It all depends on how you use it. Regardless of race, religion, gender, culture, socioeconomics, or orientation, the Enneagram can be helpful to anyone, anywhere.

Although it is not distinctly Christian, the Enneagram can be leveraged to cultivate the Christian life. That is what this book aims to do.

People often ask me how I defend the Enneagram against such accusations. I tell them not to get sucked into defending it. One either finds it helpful or doesn't. It is neither salvific nor soul destroying. It's simply a tool. From that standpoint it can be leveraged just as Paul leveraged an "unknown god" in Acts 17 to spur his listeners on to accept the claims of the gospel. God uses every square inch. If God can use an unknown god to amplify the name of Jesus, God can surely use the Enneagram.

I affirm the words of pastor and author Adele Calhoun on the Enneagram: "It is not Jesus." It is not the solution to life's riddles. It is not the decoder of the deep mysteries. It is not "your best life now."

But as a tool, it has proven to be incredibly useful in revealing what motivates our behavior as humans and in showing whether our choices are leading to health and wholeness.

Augmented Reality

The Enneagram acts as a lens, a kind of augmented reality, if you will. This is not the same thing as virtual reality. In virtual reality, one puts on an entire apparatus and is transported through vision to a different context. Virtual reality leads us into fantasy. Augmented reality, rather than transporting you out of your context, aims to provide helpful information about the current context. So think of the Enneagram as a pair of augmented-reality glasses. As we put them on, we begin to see our lives through a lens. This lens helps us become increasingly aware of what is motivating our actions while also understanding that the people around us may be motivated differently than we are. This means that the Enneagram, when properly used as a lens, can both increase our self-awareness and foster compassion for others. It is obvious, then, why the Enneagram can become useful in family relationships, marriage, leadership, and personal growth.

As a lens, the Enneagram helps us notice our patterns of behavior. The nine personality types of the Enneagram, the Enneatypes, capture the basic default patterns of human personality. We all have within us each of the nine types, but each of us tends toward one type more than the others. This is called your "core type" or "core personality." Those well versed in the Enneagram will notice in the main text of this book the absence of intricacies such as wings, triads, subtypes, and other aspects of the theory that make it wonderfully complex. In the appendix, I have included some brief material on these subjects, as well as resources for exploring these nuances in more detail. The purpose of this book is to explore a basic knowledge of the Enneagram for deeper Christian living.

Four Agreements

When I lead Enneagram workshops, I ask participants to make the following four agreements, which are worth mentioning from the outset here as well:

1. **Remember that you are not a number.** Your core personality is not synonymous with your root identity. Your personality is a survival strategy (often subconscious) to thrive and cope in a beautiful and broken world.

2. **Refuse to become branded as the Enneagram person, church, or organization.** The Enneagram is a great tool, but it should always remain in the background and never become the foreground that defines a community or organization. When the language of the Enneagram becomes the normative social jargon, newcomers will experience exclusion.

3. **Resist the urge to type another person.** We each have the privilege of making our own journey of self-discovery. Furthermore, the Enneagram is a motives theory, and none of us has access to anyone else's motives. We are able to see others' behavior, but this does not provide us with enough data to type someone. Just

because you know the Enneagram does not mean you know the person across the table.

4. **Reclaim the Enneagram as a means, not an end.** Like a pair of glasses we put on to see life with increased self-awareness and compassion, the Enneagram is a tool to help us move toward growth.

Personal and Communal

Before moving on to chapter 1, here are a couple of thoughts to consider from a distinctly Christian perspective. In the Christian imagination, each type—when operating in health—reveals an aspect of God. One reason the Enneagram is sometimes referred to as the nine faces of the soul is that each type reflects a different dimension of the *imago Dei*. Whereas many (wrongly) view the Enneagram from an individualist perspective, what it means for Christians is that we reflect the nature of God better together than we do apart. It takes a community of diverse personalities coming together to present a fuller picture of the Divine to the world. In this way, the Enneagram makes a case for the necessity of the local church.

Just as we are a temple built out of living stones (1 Pet. 2:5) and spiritual gifts (1 Cor. 12:7ff.), our unique personalities function to express the breadth of God. Since each of us will resonate with one core type more than the others, the Enneagram is an invitation to surround ourselves with others who are motivated differently than we are, and to see the beauty of God's diversity in the vastness of human personality. Truly, we need each other to fully express God in the world.

The second thought to consider revolves around nature versus nurture. Inevitably during my workshops, someone will ask: Was I born a Nine (or a Two, or whatever number), or did I become a Nine along the way? I am hesitant to answer this definitively because neither genetics nor psychology or sociology are my fields of expertise. That said, with no small ounce of humility, I invite the learner to consider that both play a factor.

We are born with genetic dispositions that lend themselves to particular behaviors. For example, I observe many similarities between Nines and Twos. I often see similarities between Eights, Sevens, Threes, and so on. Genetic coding probably has something to do with these similarities in behavioral patterns. However, through life experiences those personality proclivities become concretized, and thus a core personality becomes solidified in us. Remember, your personality is a strategy to cope and thrive in the world. At some point in life, our personality begins to form (some refer to this as putting on a mask) as a strategy to succeed or to survive. One cannot underestimate the contribution that both nature and nurture play in human personality.

As you journey through *The Enneagram for Spiritual Formation*, may you know above all else that you are beloved. The same God who created you is the God who is committed to you—in all your beauty and all your brokenness. May you know that transformation is always available, because the One who is renewing the world is ever present within the core of your being.

Anyone who asks, "Do you know who I am?" needs to
be prepared to hear the answer, "No—do you?"

—Samuel Wells

Now the Lord is the Spirit, and where the Spirit of the
Lord is, there is freedom. And we all, who with unveiled
faces contemplate the Lord's glory, are being transformed into his image with ever-increasing glory, which
comes from the Lord, who is the Spirit.

—2 Corinthians 3:17–18

SKEPTIC'S QUESTION: **Is my personality the same thing
as my identity?**

RESPONSE: **No—but sort of.**

I hate the Enneagram. (And even as I write that, I can hear my mother's voice reminding me that "hate" is such a strong word.) Let me explain. When I say that I hate the Enneagram, what I mean is that I don't like what it has become for many, which includes the following:

a reduction of the self to a number

a strategy to box in other people

a secret language that creates insiders and outsiders

identity rooted in belovedness

an end rather than a means

a superficial parlor trick rather than a key to unlocking self-awareness

And the list could go on. These are just a few of the land mines I've encountered while teaching workshops on the Enneagram and Christian formation all over the world. Through these workshops, I have formed this central conviction: you are not a number.

So who are you? This is the perennial question.

The movie *Zoolander* has a scene that perfectly portrays this. In a fit of existential crisis, model Derek Zoolander, played by Ben Stiller, storms out of a building and into a parking lot. His ego has been deflated through a series of unfortunate events. We've all been there. Staring down, he gazes into a street puddle that reflects his image back to him. When he asks, "Who am I?" his alter ego unexpectedly replies, "I don't know." His conclusion? "I guess I have a lot of things to ponder."

Identity is complicated. And we all have a lot of things to ponder, especially in a society that constantly tosses us dehumanizing life scripts with which to define ourselves.

But the truth is, the foundation of your being is *not*:

your personality	your race
your career	your income
your gender	your gifts
your sexuality	your talents

Just take a step back and breathe. Let that reality sink in for a moment.

And then, hear this: While these characteristics are important, and they do somehow coincide with or stem from your identity, beneath them lies a deeper essence, something that is true about you even before you discover all that good stuff, something even more foundational to your existence than your childhood wound, or your skin pigment, or your passion for mint chocolate-chip ice cream.

Let's imagine your whole existence through the metaphor of a tree. Think of your identity not as the visible characteristics mentioned above but as the root system that runs beneath what is visible about you to the world.

Figure 1

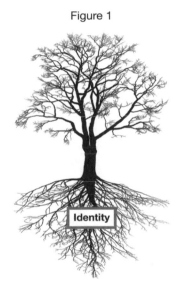

So who are you? What is your identity?

According to the Hebrew Scriptures (what Christians know as the Old Testament), underneath it all, every single human who has ever lived and will ever exist is an image bearer of the Creator-God. This is both unavoidable and unchangeable. The Judeo-Christian understanding of identity is utterly obvious in the early writings of Genesis. Rather than teasing the reader through dramatic suspense, the writer quickly settles the matter of identity on page 1 of the Bible:

> So God created mankind in his own image,
>   in the image of God he created them;
>   male and female he created them. (Gen. 1:27)

When Scripture declares this over the first humans, they had yet to contribute anything (good or bad) to the world. They were *imago Dei* (image of God) at their root before manifesting anything visibly in the world.

This means the ground of identity is hardwired as *being*, not *doing*—which makes me think the world we live in might be messed up, since that contradicts the societal script we are given from childhood.

The New Testament affirms the Genesis declaration but says it in a different way. To be made in God's image is to be *agapētos*—beloved. Echoing Genesis, the writer of the First Gospel, Mark, doesn't waste any time teasing the reader through dramatic suspense about the identity of Jesus. In Mark 1, Jesus is baptized in the Jordan River: "Just as Jesus was coming up out of the water, he saw heaven being torn open and the Spirit descending on him like a dove. And a voice came from heaven: 'You are my Son, whom I love [*agapētos*]; with you I am well pleased'" (vv. 10–11).

It's as if a new creation, in Jesus of Nazareth, is beginning here at this moment. Maybe this is why Paul later described him as the second Adam (Rom. 5). But it does leave the reader wondering *why* the Father is pleased with the Son. At this point in his life, Jesus has done little worth mentioning, according to Mark. Baptism marks the ministerial entry point of Jesus into the world. It is the event that inaugurates and commissions his vocation. And the title of "beloved" is given to him before he preaches any sermons, calls any disciples, or performs consistent miracles throughout Judea. In other words, God gives him this name not as a result of getting anything done but because it is the original intent of the human condition, *imago Dei*.

Imago Dei as Belovedness

Belovedness is not dependent on personality, gifting, or any of the characteristics listed above. Belovedness simply *is*. We are beloved because we are made in the image of God. Jesus patterns for us this most significant truth—identity is received, not achieved. What does this mean? It means we must always resist the temptation to reduce identity to anything less than the image of God.

Again, your identity is not reducible to a number. You are a mystery who is deeply beloved by a mysterious God who came in flesh and showed us the fullest expression of what it means to be truly human. You were made to remind God of God; hence, you reflect God's image. *That* is who you are. And in your belovedness, like a strong root system, you are resilient.

Day after day, I repeat the same message to my daughter, hoping it will dig deep tire tracks of truth into her neural pathways:

Me: Eloise! Did you know there is nothing you can do to make me love you any more?

Eloise (*slightly annoyed*): Yes, Dad.

Me: And did you know there is nothing you can do to make me love you any less?

Eloise (*slightly more annoyed*): Yes, Dad.

Both of us together: I love you that I love you that I love you.

This is as close as I can get to imagining how God relates to us. Every single day my greatest task is to begin the day basking in the awesome reality that my belovedness is not up for negotiation. My belovedness to God does not change season to season, day to day, moment to moment. God's unwavering commitment to our shared eternity is not dependent on my actions but is predetermined by him. In a world of conditional love, shallow commitments, and broken promises, this is an earth-shattering truth. The love the Father pronounced over the Son at baptism is the same love that is transferred onto God's children. That's crazy!

Henri Nouwen, the late Catholic priest and scholar, is one of my spiritual heroes. He believed that we, at the foundational level of our being, "are the beloved sons and daughters of God."[1] Jesus models at his baptism what is also true of us. Before performing works, God pronounces words. Before we achieve anything, we receive everything. Our identity is not earned, but given! To answer Philip Yancey's question in the title of his best-selling book, *this* is what's so amazing about grace.[2] When we live from the place of rooted identity, health and wholeness become possible in our personality. Your personality, wounds and all, can then become a gift to the world around you. This is where the Enneagram is helpful.

What Is Personality?

Although your identity is never reduced to your personality, the two are connected. Like the root system of a tree, the roots are not the stem, but neither can they be severed. Therefore, the greater that one believes in their inherent belovedness, the healthier one's personality should be. But because it is challenging to receive this divine gift, we end up strategizing, manipulating, and coercing to get approval, affection, and acceptance everywhere we turn.

What, then, is personality? Generally speaking, personality is a well-forged *strategy* to both thrive and cope in a beautiful and broken world. Personality is unique to every person. The nine types of the Enneagram are various motivational patterns that emerge as a strategy to thrive and cope. However, like a fingerprint, no two people on earth have the exact same personality. We are far too wonderfully and mysteriously made to be totalized by and reduced to a number on a diagram. Personality, then, is the outgrowth—the stem, if you will—from which our identity flows. Personality is forged by both our unique genetic makeup and our diverse life experiences (nature and nurture). Over time we begin to form patterns of behavior that reflect nine types.

Figure 2

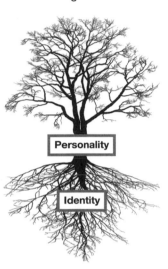

Think of it this way: Your *identity* is the beloved image of God; this is given and universally true. Your *personality* is forged; this is particular and unique to you. The Enneagram helps us map nine patterns of behavior that are common to all people throughout the world, while also preserving the uniqueness of every person who has ever lived, including you.

Character and Gifts

What begins with a root system called *identity* is then filtered through one's personality. Although every number is in every person, each person "presents" one dominant type out of the nine more so than he or she presents the others (more on this in the next chapter). Keep in mind that theories such as the Enneagram are helpful, but they are not final. In an art metaphor, the Enneagram is more like an impressionist painting than a documentary photograph. From afar, the nine types put us in touch with a general image, but up close they each break down because the human condition is far too complex to be reduced to a number within a motives theory. Nevertheless, the Enneagram is incredibly helpful and worthwhile for self-awareness that can help us grow.

From our identity and personality we then develop integrity of character (or lack thereof) and also various gifts (or talents) that eventually manifest in the world. What others experience of you is largely what they experience from your gifts and character. When we live from a rooted identity and seek health in our personality, our character and gifts contribute to the flourishing of the world. When we are not rooted in identity and are not healthy in personality, the opposite of flourishing manifests in and through our lives. Spiritual formation matters.

Human beings attempt to compensate when we sense that our identities are unsettled. At that point personality overreaches and attempts to fill the void. This explains, for instance, why some seek accomplishment (Threes) and others seek service (Twos). Some strive for perfection (Ones), while others retreat into their analytical selves as a protection strategy (Fives). These are all attempts to secure our identity. But the gospel reminds us that we are already beloved and that we do not have to earn that gift through our personality.

The behaviors that manifest from our personalities are typically subconscious motivations that result in what many refer to as our "shadow side," a psychological term for the parts of ourselves that we don't want to admit to having and that remain unnamed. When we're unhealthy, we're often unaware of the ways we manipulate, coerce, or disengage from the world, causing us to behave in patterns that are not good for ourselves or others. The fruits of our shadow side are more like weeds, we could say—weeds that inflict harm and cause damage, sometimes even to the point of spiritual and relational death.

Weeds of the ego are worth mentioning here, because they are often omitted when Christians talk about fruit of the Spirit. The fruits of the Spirit are found toward the end of Paul's letter to the Galatians. They are the character (or virtues) the church is collectively called to manifest in order to reveal the character of God. They are "love, joy, peace, forbearance, kindness, goodness, faithfulness, gentleness and self-control" (Gal. 5:22–23). Prior to this text, Paul mentions a set of characteristics that do not manifest the character of God but do just the opposite. These are the weeds of the ego. They manifest most when we do not believe our belovedness and then misuse personality as a strategy to thrive and cope in ways that are misaligned with God's kingdom. These weeds, according to Paul, are "sexual immorality, impurity and debauchery; idolatry and witchcraft; hatred, discord, jealousy, fits of rage, selfish ambition, dissensions, factions and envy; drunkenness, orgies, and the like" (vv. 19–21).

Figure 3

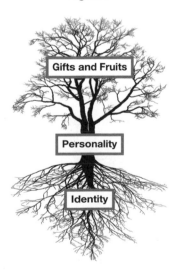

It is critical, then, that we daily reclaim our inherent beloved-ness; otherwise, we will use others and shame ourselves because of our perceived inadequacy and unlovability. From this emerges the primary purpose of spiritual practices in the Christian life: to reconnect us with the presence of God and the gift of others. Within these practices or habits we can reclaim what it is that God says is already true at our root. With prescient clarity, Nouwen often repeated that we are trapped in three pernicious lies. These lies aim to detach us from our belovedness and wreak havoc in our personalities:

1. I am what I have.

2. I am what I do.

3. I am what other people say or think about me.[3]

When these lies are at play within us, we will be improperly motivated. Each Enneagram type succumbs to different strategies in an effort to fix what we feel is broken or supply what we sense is lacking. The most tragic part of all is when we discover that in the ocean of God's immeasurable goodness, we are never lacking for that which we most need.

To sum up, we begin with our grace-given identity, not our developing personality. Our identity is beloved, and this is given as a gift from God. We then move confidently into expressing our belovedness in the world, uniquely, through personality. And our personalities then manifest in the forms of character and gifts.

The Tree of Life

So far I've used a tree metaphor to talk in broad strokes about being human. I've tried to correlate the following:

Roots = Identity

Stem = Personality

Limbs and leaves = Character and gifts

Permit me to take the metaphor one step further. In Genesis, God eliminates the possibility of the humans eating from the Tree of Life as a grace to prevent them from living eternally in the sin nature (Gen. 3:22). The next place in Scripture where the Tree of Life emerges is Revelation 22:2. This is the same tree that God took away from the garden in Genesis. But at the end of days, in the coming resurrection and renewal of all things, a river flows from the throne of God down to the Tree of Life, which bears fruit. The text is rather mysterious because on either side of the river stands the tree.

The reason I bring up the Tree of Life is that the Scriptures begin and end with it. The narrative God wants to tell is about life. Life is the theme of the entire Bible. Creation teems with life. Cain takes life. In the Hebrew Scriptures (the Old Testament), God gives commands in order that the people of Israel would "choose life" (Deut. 30:19). In the Gospels, Jesus declares, "I am the way and the truth and the life" (John 14:6). Those in the Son will be raised to everlasting life. God is in the business of life. The Scriptures begin and end with the Tree of Life. Don't miss the plot. The big story is life!

A Tree Called Your Life

From Genesis to Revelation, the story God is telling is one of cosmic proportion. The Tree of Life is shorthand for this plot. But within that cosmic story we are also summoned to a personal story—a story of transformation. This personal journey is the tree we have been illustrating thus far—identity, personality, and gifts/fruits. This is not the Tree of Life, but rather *a tree called your life*. There are two parallel journeys happening simultaneously. As you consent toward the larger one, you will inevitably transform the smaller one.

You are a kind of ecosystem. God has made you in the divine image, and you present a personality in the world in order to cope and thrive, even as you are called to manifest character gifts for the good of the world. The quest I am inviting you on through this book is one where we seek to transform a tree called your life into optimal health for the sake of the world. As we commit to this, we will be on the ancient path toward the Tree of Life we find in Scripture.

Are you with me?

In almost every Enneagram workshop I've led, at least a handful of participants shed tears of shame, pain, and despair when discovering their type for the first time. They attest to feeling "caught" as their personality patterns are explained by the Enneagram typing system. We are largely unaware of the default motives that drive our behaviors. These motives hide themselves deep in our neural pathways. Therefore, when someone else names what has been (strategically and subconsciously) hidden, it is like taking a shovel to the soul and bringing the dirt of one's life up to the surface. In that moment, self-awareness rises to the surface, and the tears of shame roll down. You feel existentially naked, like someone is reading a secretive journal you write while sleeping but forget about when you wake. It can be embarrassing at best and emotionally devastating at worst.

This may help explain why some prefer to stay away from the Enneagram. People often use cover stories like "It's too New Agey," or "It's so cliché," or "I don't want to be reduced to a type," and so on. Sometimes those are just excuses made to avoid one's shadow side. Sitting with brokenness and recognizing the need to do deep self-work takes vulnerability. Through the Enneagram, our "life junk" emerges from the shadows that we often prefer to leave in the dark. And it is here, amid that darkness and devastation, that the Christian faith reconstructs human life. This is precisely what inspired me to get involved with spiritual formation utilizing the Enneagram as a tool. The Enneagram leads us into naming our shadow and increasing our self-awareness. Once we do this, we can step into the light of Christ and move into life transformation.

In Christ

The phrase "in Christ" (Greek: *en Christō*) saturates the New Testament. Depending on your Bible translation, it is used between seventy-five and one hundred times. "In Christ" designates the sphere or domain to which one joyfully surrenders their small story. To live in Christ is to desire to bring your small story under the larger framework of Christ's lordship. Whenever the choice to surrender is made, being in Christ works on us at every level—identity, personality, and gifts.

In Christ, we can fully recognize and receive the image of God in which we were made. In Christ, we may access our belovedness at the deepest level. In Christ, we are opened to the redemptive, indwelling presence of the Holy Spirit, who cultivates maturity over time within our personalities. In Christ, the Holy Spirit imparts unique gifts to build up the church and the world. As it relates to the Enneagram, in Christ the broken patterns of our personalities can be transformed. This is one way in which tools like the Enneagram serve as a lens to help us see what we are prone to (sub)consciously avoid. Broken patterns of behavior—manifesting from wounded motives—can be healed and set free as we participate in the divine life (2 Pet. 1:4). Being in Christ revives us at every level of our being. We need the external resource of God in order to become who God says we fully are.

Figure 4

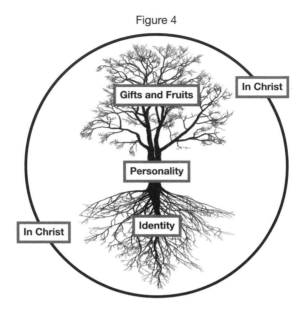

The "in Christ" dynamic functions as the answer to some of life's most daunting questions, such as:

Can I become whole despite my fragmented and broken self?

Is it possible to live from my beloved identity and not from deep insecurity?

Can I grow into health within my personality? If so, where would I begin?

How can I change patterns of behavior that are prone to addiction?

All of these questions share a common answer: Yes, in Christ! If we are to develop a Christian understanding of being human, it must not only include but make central the presence of the living Christ as *the* transformative agent who makes formation possible. "In Christ" is the tangible way of saying deep grace. In Christ,

God was not content for grace to remain abstract and distant. Grace is not an ambiguous gift. Grace has come to the world specifically and historically in the form of Jesus of Nazareth. The mystery of his life, death, and resurrection is imparted freely to willing humans through the person of the Holy Spirit. Within this dynamic, our identity (roots), personality (stem), and character and gifts (limbs and leaves) start to thrive.

Time and time again, in the Christian story we discover the depths of our belovedness only as we paradoxically die to self and rise with him. Christ's life becomes our life, for "to live is Christ and to die is gain" (Phil. 1:21). Christ's story is now our story. His future is our future. His cosmic death and resurrection brings hope to our individual deaths and longings toward resurrection. To be *in Christ*, by faith, means to take our small stories and tuck them into the fabric of Christ's metastory. The New Testament consistently reminds us to root our identity *in Christ*, not in our temporary successes or failures. For example, in the first two chapters of Ephesians, *in Christ* we

> have been chosen and adopted by the Father (1:4–6)
>
> have been redeemed by the Son (1:7–12)
>
> have been sealed with the Spirit (1:13–14)
>
> have been given resurrection power (1:19)
>
> have been given eyes to see the lordship of Jesus (1:15–23)
>
> have been brought from death to life by grace through faith (2:1–10)
>
> have been raised and seated with him in the heavens (2:5–7)
>
> have been created for good works (2:10)[4]

Twentieth-century theologian Karl Barth said it well when teaching the letter to the Ephesians to his Göttingen theology students in 1921: "What I am, I am in relation to God."[5] Personhood, in the Christian life, is best discovered when surrendered and is most lost when clutched and clung to. This is the challenging paradox of Christianity.

Theologian Robert Mulholland explains that there are two choices of self-understanding according to the Christian faith. One is trusting in our own resources and abilities. The other is trusting radically in God. Mulholland writes that you "cannot be grasped or sustained in the deeper life in God—being like Jesus—until you are awakened at the deep levels of your being to this essential reality."[6] This essential reality is consistent with being *in Christ*, which is to surrender to God's deep grace and not be dependent on our human resources for self-worth, approval, or identity. Paul's famous line is worth repeating here: "I have been crucified with Christ and I no longer live, but Christ lives in me. The life I now live in the body, I live by faith in the Son of God, who loved me and gave himself for me" (Gal. 2:20).

In surrendering to the person of Christ, our transformation becomes most possible. The life of Christ within us transforms our identity, reconnecting us with our inherent belovedness and healing our personalities so that we may be driven by good desires and may manifest spiritual fruit through our gifts, words, and various contributions to a broken world. The life of Christ completely encircles our lives, healing us from within and transforming us without. Figure 4 helps us understand how being in Christ functions as an orbit around us in life, healing us at every turn.

Self-understanding and transformation open to their fullest human capacity in Christ. To be sure, one can attain measures of self-awareness without the in-Christ dynamic. But in-Christ humans are no longer limited by the dominion of evil and the power of sin. Grace works deep.

In Christ, we have redemption and full access to our belovedness because he takes our shame to the cross. In Christ, we have increased transformative power to heal our personalities because his resurrection power works in us. In Christ, we have increased fruitfulness and gifts because he gives kingdom authority to those who believe in him. I do not write this with the intent of excluding those outside the Christian faith. I write this because the cosmic mystery—first revealed millennia ago in the Middle East and then scattered to all the world—is that the restoration of the human condition transpires in Christ. By being nailed to a tree of death on Golgotha, Jesus reestablishes the Tree of Life from the garden.

I leave the final words of this chapter as a blessing over you:

Who am I, you ask? You are a beloved child of God, made in the divine image. May you receive your divine identity from God, in Christ, through the Spirit, and reject the false self that wants to reduce your worth to superficial attachments and trivial appetites.

practice

Take a few minutes to meditate on the wisdom of the passage below. The writer seeks to be reminded here of the mystery of God's creation—namely, the human being. Remember: you are not a number, you are not reducible, and you are the beloved creation of God, made in God's image to reflect that image back into the world.

Set your timer for five minutes, and whisper these words again and again until they find a grip on your mind, your emotions, and the deepest parts of who you are:

> So God created mankind in his own image,
> in the image of God he created them;
> male and female he created them.
> Genesis 1:27

2

Be yourself; everyone else is already taken.

—Oscar Wilde

I praise you because I am fearfully and wonderfully
  made;
 your works are wonderful,
 I know that full well.

—Psalm 139:14

> **SKEPTIC'S QUESTION: Am I only one type on the Enneagram?**
>
> **RESPONSE: You have all the types in you, but you have a dominant Enneatype (or pattern) that does not change through the course of life.**

love the Enneagram. "Love is for people, not things," my mother-in-law says. I wouldn't say I love the Enneagram like I love my family. But the Enneagram has been a tremendous gift that has unlocked many doors inside myself that felt stuck and caused me frustration as a follower of Jesus. I love the Enneagram like I love a deep bowl of Tonkotsu Ramen. I mean, I wouldn't die for it . . . probably.

In chapter 1, I teased out the differences between root identity and core personality. Succinctly put, our identity lies at the root of ourselves, and our personality is the stem that emerges from the root. Personality is a

personality how we cope in a harsh world

37

strategy to cope and thrive in a beautiful and broken world. There are times when our personalities work to our benefit, advancing our desires, relationships, and convictions. There are other times when our personalities work against us, isolating us from others, preventing our hopes from being realized, and repeating cycles of self-condemnation. Every personality constantly shifts between health and unhealth. Our personalities operate largely on a subconscious level—meaning, we are often unaware of the motives driving our behaviors. Personality, in this sense, sometimes functions like a sort of autopilot mode that moves us through the world.

The Enneagram is a tool that helps us see our default patterns of behavior and become conscious of what's driving our lives. It is a motives theory, revealing what drives our behaviors, what lies underneath all the stuff that everyone sees. Imagine personality as an iceberg.

Figure 5

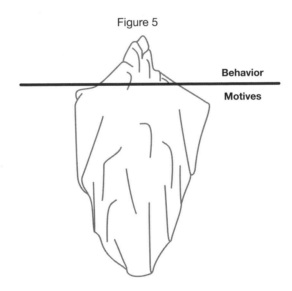

As the iceberg image in figure 5 makes clear, our motives—those unseen drivers of human behavior—are no small thing. In fact, one might say that behaviors are simply the outgrowth of motives. Motives are at the base of the iceberg of life, invisible to others and often unknown (or only subconsciously known) even to ourselves. Behavior, then, is how our motives are manifested in the world—they lie above the surface of the water and are what others experience from us.

Becoming Self-Aware

On that spring afternoon in 2013, as Father Rohr read aloud descriptions of each Enneagram type, what he said about the Three struck me. I could feel my heartbeat accelerate, my palms sweating, and anxiety creeping in. It was as if he were reading my journal. I later asked him privately, "How do you know that you know your core type?" He replied, "When you feel the highest amount of humiliation."

When I feel the highest amount of humiliation? Yikes.

It's easy to understand why some people prefer to keep a safe distance from the Enneagram. It can be rather humiliating, as if someone just named what you spent a lifetime trying to conceal. All your silly, subconscious life strategies are revealed to yourself and others. It is not uncommon for participants in my workshops to break down and weep when reading about their core type. This is why the Enneagram must never be misused as a parlor trick to impress others with our knowledge, or as a way of shrinking ourselves and others to a number. Rather, it is always a means to a transformative breakthrough. Everything begins with self-awareness. Once we see and name what lies underneath, we can bring it out into the open and begin to strategize pathways toward wholeness.

Don't miss the plot here. God can use all the raw materials of life—even humiliation—to bring about new revelation. Maybe this is partly what Paul meant when he wrote that God works all things together for good for those who love him according to God's purpose (Rom. 8:28). Remember, you are resiliently beloved in the eyes of God. That is who you are. Nothing can change that. No number on the Enneagram, no amount of health or unhealth, can ever nullify the image of God within you. God loves you that God loves that God loves you! This enables you to face whatever is revealed with courage and not despair.

Getting back to the iceberg analogy, much of your personality is unseen. Suzanne Stabile, an Enneagram expert and author, wisely said in a 2015 workshop I attended, "Just because you know the Enneagram does not mean you know the person standing right in front of you." This means that two humans can behave the exact same way yet be driven by opposite motives. Discovering your core type, then, is your own journey to make, not someone else's. No one else has access to your motives. No one but you can truly know what is driving your behavior. This requires self-awareness, and the Enneagram specializes in waking us up to ourselves.

Discerning Your Type

Waking up to ourselves doesn't typically happen in a sudden flash of insight; it is a process, a journey. To that end, the remainder of this chapter attempts to offer tools for your own journey, beginning with three steps for discerning your Enneagram type, and followed by a brief description of each type. The appendix, as I noted in the introduction, contains resources on various rabbit trails that you may choose (if you're anything like me) to gleefully skip down and explore. The purpose of this book is to outline the Enneagram's basic typology so that you can move beyond type and into Christian living. If nothing from this book has stuck with you yet, read these words from Karl Barth and allow them to sink in for a moment: "The ultimate aim of our personality is that it can become a gift and not a lord; a servant and not a master."[1] Transformation is available. Discipleship is essential. And as my dear friend Jamie Tworkowski likes to say, "Rescue is possible."

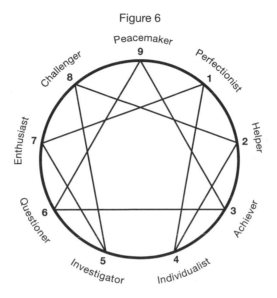

Figure 6

Discerning your type will require some focused effort and attention. Following are three steps to help guide you in your own discernment process:

1. Read through the descriptions of the types below. Is there one type that brings more humiliation than the others?

2. Narrow your focus to several core types. Read the descriptions on either side of your core types. If you have narrowed down your types, say, to One and Five, notice the numbers next to each of these (for One, this means taking a closer look at Nine and Two; for Five, this means taking a closer look at Four and Six). These adjacent numbers are called "wings" and are usually written as, for example, 1w9 (for a One with a Nine wing). We

each typically lean one direction or another. Considering whether you are prone to move toward a wing type can help you discern your core type.

3. Invite a few people who know you well into your discernment process. Bounce your initial types off of them and ask for input. Although others do not know your motives, they can be helpful in the process of self-discovery.

The Nine Types

> **Type One**
>
> **One word:** Perfectionist
> **Four words:** Idealist, principled, independent, critical
> **Survival strategy:** "I must be perfect and good."[2]

Ones need to feel justified by their conscience before they can act. Ones struggle to relate to their environment because of the incessant need for perfection before acting. They are dissatisfied with the way the world currently is and seek an idealized state. Extremely principled with strong convictions, they are also dissatisfied with their own imperfection within the imperfect world, and they live toward the way things "ought" to be.

They also fear making a mistake, which often leaves them immobile. Average Ones (and by "average" here I simply mean somewhere between healthy and unhealthy, mature and immature) become angry and frustrated easily when their surrounding environment does not cooperate with their standard of perfection and processes.[3] They are ideologues.

From an early age, Ones learned to behave properly.[4] Often their natural desires were forbidden as children, so they block desire in order to do the right thing. They sometimes recall being painfully criticized. As a result, they learned to monitor themselves to avoid mistakes that would come to others' attention. Like the Puritans, they work hard, are independent, and can be self-righteous.[5] They are convinced that life is hard and that ease is earned. They understand delayed gratification better than any other type.

Severely compulsive, they believe there is always room for improvement. If the world is under an alien invasion, they are cleaning their bathroom because they can at least take control of that situation. They are critical, but procrastinate out of fear of getting it wrong or making a mistake. Comparison is brutal for Ones, and social media can be emotionally crippling because they perceive themselves as inadequate when viewing others' posts.

Often good teachers, Ones strive to set healthy examples of the way things "ought" to be. They tend to be model children who are motivated to "be good," "try harder," and "get it right." Morally, behaviorally, and vocationally, they are dissatisfied with the state of things. From an early age they sought perfection out of fear of losing the love of their dear ones. They are often gifted children who are later viewed as "anal-retentive." It is a heavy thing to be a One because they are relentlessly embattled in inner trials. They chase discounts and clean rooms, are committed to duty, and disappoint themselves by their own imperfection. This often leads them to inner anger.[6]

Ones experience life as a burden. They often repress anger because the world (and themselves) is not what it should be. They see through idealized glasses. They are desperate to be correct and right. They suffer from a relentless inner critic. When they are criticized by others, they experience this as a severe blow that serves to reinforce their own inner critic. They are good at perfecting things when the world is not going well. When they experience a situation that is out of their control (for example, if a loved one is sick), they clean their house, motivated by the need to perfect something within their realm of control. They best operate from within strict, clear guidelines, feedback, and a single course of action.[7] They suppress anger so that when it does surface it is usually related to something deeper.

> **The lie Ones believe:** "It's not okay to make a mistake."
> **The truth Ones need:** "You are good."[8]

Type Two

One word: Helper

Four words: Relational, generous, insecure, self-forgetful

Survival strategy: "I must be helpful and caring."

At their best, Twos are healing presences in the world.[9] Service is very important to Twos. They move toward others, but at the same time are often subconsciously motivated by self-interest. Further, they rarely notice their own insecurity when doing this because they are unself-aware. The average Two does more talking about serving others than actually serving others. Helen Palmer notes that Twos "are marked by the need for affection and approval; they want to be loved, protected and feel important in others' lives."[10] They develop a keen perception of others' moods and preferences and then act accordingly. Twos easily alter their own tastes and preferences to serve the desires of others. This gives rise to what Palmer calls the "multiple self."[11] They can be characterized as so in tune with the feelings of others that they lose touch with their own. Over time, this can lead Twos to have trouble discerning personal longings and preferences.

"Twos have an exaggerated need for validation."[12] They are prone to flattery and giving public approval of others for personal purposes. Some Twos report that early in life they had to provide care and support for both older and younger members of the family. Because of this, they develop a "need to be needed," which results in secret pride. Even though they are extremely helpful, they expect (and often demand) gratitude in return.[13]

At the root, immature Twos struggle with identity, which is why they invest their resources in others, hoping their acknowledgment and gratitude will fill the void. Describing how immature Twos are prone to function in committed relationships, Palmer claims, "The early phases of a relationship are dominated by a Two living out those aspects that will flatter the partner's needs. The later phases of a relationship are dominated by the feelings of being controlled by the partner's will, coupled by an overwhelming desire for freedom. Twos experience a conflict between the habit of molding self-presentation so as to be ultimately irresistible to a partner and wanting the freedom to do whatever they please."[14]

In the end, Twos gain control through helpfulness, believing that others need them in order to thrive. However, they want recognition of their usefulness, lest they become insecure and angry. Their twin preoccupations are gaining approval and avoiding rejection. They take subversive pride in their assistance, to the extent that they hope others will not be able to get along without them. Twos can be so thoroughly others-oriented that if they are not needed, they believe themselves to be unwanted. Questions Twos should ask themselves before serving others: What is my agenda? What is the return? Does this person want my help?

The lie Twos believe: "It's not okay to have my own needs."
The truth Twos need: "You are wanted."

Type Three

One word: Achiever
Four words: Image-conscious, ambitious, adaptable, motivated
Survival strategy: "I must be impressive and attractive."[15]

The axiom of the Three is to avoid failure and maximize success. Threes are often out of touch with their own feelings because they are busy shaping others' impressions of them. Adept in agility, they can adapt to whatever is needed in the moment to ensure success, security, and social assimilation. Above all, they seek to project a desirable image.[16] Unlike the Two, who asks, "Do you like me?" the Three asks, "Am I successful?"[17] As children, Threes were prized for their achievements. Thus, their proclivities are learned from and reinforced by guardians.

Threes recall feeling worth through performance and image rather than through emotional and social connectedness. Palmer states, "Because they were loved for their achievements, they learned to suspend their own emotions and focus their attention on earning the status that would guarantee them love. It was very important to avoid failure, because only winners were worthy of love."[18]

Threes are driven by three *c*'s: competency, comparison, and competition. They are some of the most competent and efficient people in their respective fields because identity hangs in the balance. Whereas Threes work hard to develop competence, onlookers often would not know because they give the appearance of ease. They ardently compare themselves with others at the office in order to gauge their skill and expertise. And they compete to be first, to get the promotion or receive whatever award is available in order to feel worthy within their environment. Others are often unaware they are competing with a Three. But this is how a Three experiences inner validation: by winning. Threes are often called chameleons because they become whatever it takes to fit and thrive within a milieu. Threes "can slip into almost any mask and act the part to perfection."[19]

Threes thrive within a capitalistic society because both are undergirded by competency, comparison, and competition. Rohr believes that the Three grows out of affluent cultures: "I am sure that in the Third World countries, one would not meet the same percentage of Threes as in the U.S."[20] Because they are at home and valued in Western culture, they often appear optimistic and cool. According to Palmer, "They do not appear to suffer and may live out their entire life oblivious to the fact that they have lost a vital connection to their own interior life."[21] If the One values effectiveness, the Three values efficiency; if the One seeks to get things right, the Three seeks to get things done. Threes seek to achieve in record time in order to move on to the next conquest. This can take the form of degrees, positions, accomplishments, and relationships. They also move quickly from thinking to acting. Time is of the essence, and there is much to be done. Often Threes sacrifice deep imagination that comes with reflection and calculation because they move so quickly into action. Comfortable in front of the crowd, personal intimacy and relational connection often lack in Threes because they do not want to risk vulnerability or come to terms with the fact that they have neglected their inner life.

Threes are hard to read. Because they place a high value on the exterior life (image, recognition, and achievement), they often suppress their interior feelings (anger, rage, and embarrassment). Further, they struggle to read others. Like Ones, Threes fear failure. However, the Three's fear of failure is rooted in worth, and "there is nothing sadder on the Enneagram than an unsuccessful Three."[22] They have a future orientation toward life, which is why they are always aimed out at the next prize. Threes do not shrink back from self-promotion, which finds a natural outlet in today's proliferation of social media outlets and "likes." They are multitaskers and natural salespeople. Few really ever know Threes because they remain on the surface.

At their best, Threes are self-accepting, inner-directed, and authentic.[23] At their worst, Threes are deeply narcissistic and deceptive and will hurt others for personal gain.

> **The lie Threes believe:** "It's not okay to have your own feelings."
>
> **The truth Threes need:** "You are loved for yourself, not for what you do."[24]

Type Four

One word: Individualist

Four words: Dramatic, artistic, melancholic, intuitive

Survival strategy: "I must be unique and different."

From Fours, the world receives a great deal of what is good, true, and beautiful. Fours are categorized under the feeling triad (see the appendix for more on triads) and are thus driven by their emotions. These emotions can manifest in healthy and unhealthy ways; hence, the Four is often depicted as a melancholic artist. Preferring individualism, they value authenticity and can easily perceive phony manipulation in others. They seek emotional honesty and inspiration and seek to create helpful experiences for others. According to Don Richard Riso and Russ Hudson, healthy Fours want to be true to themselves and want others to also be true to themselves.[25] This is why it is easy for them to be critical when they perceive falsity in others. The words of Shakespeare's Polonius, in *Hamlet* (act 1, scene 3), capture the Four well:

> This above all: to thine ownself be true,
> And it must follow, as the night the day,
> Thou canst not then be false to any man.

There are fewer Fours than any other type.[26] As children, they were complex and needed to feel special. Their underlying childhood theme is loss. According to Palmer, "Fours remember abandonment in childhood, and as a result suffer from a sense of deprivation and loss."[27] Fours long for that which they lack and miss out on what's in front of them. Unconsciously dwelling on what is missing, they lose sight of what they actually have.[28] Palmer continues to describe scenarios of Fours accordingly: "If you get the job, you want the man. If you get the man, you want to be alone. If you are alone, you want the job and man again. Attention cycles to the best in what is missing and, by comparison, whatever is available seems dull and valueless."[29]

Fours are often moody and struggle to feel satisfied. When it comes to vocation, Fours seldom settle for routine jobs. They would rather be true to their talents and poor than be rich "sell-outs." Often their main concern is relationships, which tend to be inconsistent at best and volatile at worst. Romantically, they love the pursuit. Once in a romantic relationship they can feel bored because the quest is over. But in friendships, they are often the first to stand in solidarity with other people's pain. Fours are excellent at the Jewish practice of sitting shiva—a funeral practice in which one offers presence to another instead of answers—during the period of mourning after someone's death, and they are drawn to the season of Lent. They are attracted to extremes and can sometimes manufacture drama in order to feel alive.[30]

Fours' orientation to life is often romantic, aesthetic, and artistic.[31] This does not mean they always have musical instruments, microphones, or paintbrushes in hand—but they often do. They express their feelings through dance, music, painting, acting, and literature.[32] Fours can unlock beauty in the world for others. When they feel stuck in the real world, Fours "reinforce their sense of self through fantasy and the imagination."[33] Fours interiorize life, which can spawn self-absorption, depression, and introversion. They are also prone to have critical spirits and pervasive negativity. They must learn to discern the difference between having a critical mind (analyzing life) and having a critical spirit (negative outlook toward others).

Spiritually, Fours reject the categories of sacred and secular. They want to see both worlds come together in a coalescence of beauty and harmony. According to Rohr, they prefer symbols and dreams to mechanics and pragmatics. Although they claim to have thrown on a few clothes as they rushed out the door, their fashion is carefully selected. They want others to notice them for the way they stand out. Aesthetically attractive, Fours can also appear "esoteric, eccentric, extravagant, or exotic."[34] Possessions bring Fours little joy; they much prefer longing. In the words of Rohr, "Longing is more important than having."[35] This is why, for Fours, the pursuit of life is more satisfying than the attainment of it.

The minds of Fours can transfix on an unalterable past mistake. Their inner monologue repeats phrases like "if only . . . if only." This inner disappointment yields seasons of self-isolation. The Four may be physically with you in the room but can mentally, spiritually, and emotionally be as far from you as the moon. In an odd psychological twist, Fours can grow to be attracted to pain, loss, and darkness. When a Four feels like a failure, anger swells within. Their thoughts can easily turn morbid, and self-hatred becomes their disposition. This leads to feelings of despair, hopelessness, and self-destruction. At their most unintegrated, many Fours contemplate suicide because the interior worldview they have constructed is so heavy that they believe this must be all there is; therefore, they wonder, "What is the point of living?" Drugs and alcohol are common release valves for Fours as coping mechanisms and forms of escape.[36]

> The lie Fours believe: "It is not okay to be too functional or too happy."
>
> The truth Fours need: "You are seen and valued for who you are."

Type Five

One word: Investigator
Four words: Perceptive, detached, informed, introverted
Survival strategy: "I must be knowledgeable and equipped."

Imagine a high, impenetrable structure with tiny windows at the top.[37] This is the Five. The investigator's personality is like a castle. The windows at the top of the castle are but the tiniest openings where others can peer in. Whereas they have developed a greed for knowledge, they also seek privacy. They learned as children that the world can be dangerous and privacy stolen. Many Fives report others intruding on them at a young age, which led them to cultivate an inner world that only they could access. Many Fives also report feeling little tenderness or intimacy in childhood, which explains why they are characterized as thinkers who are out of touch with emotional resources.[38]

Fives tend to keep their lives secret because they struggle to trust others. Many of them are introverted and lead a strategic, compartmentalized life. Because Fives work so hard to acquire the depth of their knowledge base, they tend to hoard their knowledge. For them, knowledge equals power, so it is best to not give it all away. Of all the types, Fives are the most emotionally detached. This means they are able to experience a feeling and let it go. Feelings do not imprison them. They can think their way out of most predicaments.[39]

Rohr claims that Fives are prone to a kind of emptiness, which explains why they, unlike Fours, pursue fulfillment.[40] They are always in search of the next book, seminar, silent retreat, advanced degree, or self-advancement theory. They tend to enjoy travel, plotting out museums and educational places of interest. Thus, European cities are more interesting destinations for a Five than the beaches of the Caribbean. Fives are constantly preparing and equipping themselves. They believe that acquiring data and gaining the necessary knowledge and skill in the present will equip them for the future. Fives love developing their minds and will do so at the expense of engaging their bodies. Because they are mentally alert, little escapes their notice; "they value foresight and prediction."[41] Fives are devoted to mastering what they deem worthwhile and can concentrate on single projects for great lengths at a time.

One of the greatest gifts of a Five is their emotional neutrality, which they are able to apply to others. As objective experiencers of life, they make great judges because they can easily discern fact from empathy. They are thoughtful and careful in all they do. Viewing others as irrational, Fives are independent and rarely react to life. Rather, they prefer to act in their own time and only after they have thought through the best course of action. Fives prefer not to argue in real time but would rather come back to the debate days later, after they have mentally processed the issue at hand.

They are adept at making good use of time and can finish projects independently and in a timely manner. Fives seek to know boundaries, expectations, and deadlines in advance. In meetings they prefer written agendas handed out before arrival. They also like to know what time the meeting will end. They enjoy personal freedom and can have a dry sense of humor, full of wit and sarcasm. Many experience them as good listeners who like to learn from all they observe. Stabile says, "If you ask them what they 'feel' they'll tell you what they 'think.'"[42] Further, just as they are secretive about themselves, they also keep others' secrets, thus making good confessors.

Because Fives are committed intellectuals, they can become argumentative and cynical. Further, they are prone to live in the world of theory and concepts rather than pragmatism and materialism. Riso observes, "They act like 'disembodied minds,' more preoccupied with their visions and interpretations than reality, becoming high-strung and intense." At their worst, Fives can become reclusive and nihilistic.[43] Many commentators note that schizophrenic tendencies are the pathology of an unhealthy Five. Mathematical genius John Forbes Nash, portrayed by Russell Crowe in *A Beautiful Mind*, is a good example of an unhealthy Five.

Many people experience Fives as extremely loyal, lifelong friends. In the world of social media, Fives prefer not to self-promote, compete, or demonstrate superiority. They will often use social media to follow others' lives instead of displaying their own. According to Palmer, "Fives can mask feelings of superiority over those who crave recognition or success."[44] Independently wired, they often do not need the approval of others for positive self-esteem.

> **The lie Fives believe:** "You are strong enough to not need the assistance and comfort of others."
>
> **The truth Fives need:** "Your needs are not a problem."

Type Six

> **One word:** Questioner
> **Four words:** Fearful, loyal, procrastinator, committed
> **Survival strategy:** "I must be secure and safe."

At their best, Sixes are loyal friends, will act heroically for a cause, and make great contributors on a team. Yet the average Six is suspicious of others' motives, particularly due to childhood memories of being let down by authorities. As a result, Sixes either seek a protector or challenge authority, often playing devil's advocate.[45] They struggle to trust the authority that others wield. Though they find solace in the law, the military, the church, and the community, they nonetheless view with suspicion the authority figures in organizations. According to Stabile, "The world is a slippery slope full of agendas."[46] They worry about possible future events. They can even fear their own success because of the possibility of loss. With a tendency to overreact when under stress, Sixes often blow circumstances out of proportion and are perceived as edgy, angry, and pessimistic.[47]

For Sixes, the root sin is fear, which explains why they have problems with follow-through. When they are healthy, they are conscientious and commit to a larger cause. But an average Six is dogged by a history of starts and stops. They have held many jobs, initiated several degree programs, and leave behind a trail of unfinished projects. Sixes frequently find good excuses to not continue in one trajectory. Once they begin a project, they question it. Procrastination is common in Sixes. They live with anxiety and self-doubt and, as a result, find it easier to question than to act. Sixes are cognitively driven and reason out ways to avoid possible dangers.

As part of the thinking triad (see the appendix for more on triads), the Six is more inclined toward thinking than doing. According to Palmer, "The antiauthoritarian stance makes Sixes gravitate toward underdog causes."[48] Believing that most people are manipulative, they rarely receive compliments given. Rooted in fear, they constantly scan their environment for signs of danger, easily perceiving falsity and power plays in others. A Six at their worst is paranoid. Sixes need significant time to develop trust, but they are often committed to long marriages because of their tendency to "take on the problem in the marriage."[49] Unhealthy Sixes easily project their own feelings onto others. A Six who contemplates infidelity, for example, will often assume their partner does too, as a result of projecting their own insecurities onto the other person.[50]

Of all the types, Sixes are the most complex. There are two kinds of Sixes, according to Palmer: phobic and counterphobic. Whereas some Sixes play into their personality type (phobic), others fight it (counterphobic). Most Sixes find that they can easily slide from phobic to counterphobic, depending on circumstances. This makes Sixes the most agile of all the types. Palmer writes, "A phobic type will vacillate, replacing action with analysis, filled with contradiction and self-doubt, . . . [but when operating as] counter-phobic, will overcompensate fear by becoming the sky-diving champion in order to master his fear of heights."[51]

Phobic Sixes are characterized by cowardice. Counterphobic Sixes take unnecessary risks.[52] This complexity makes Sixes hard to spot, particularly because counterphobic Sixes can be mistaken for Eights. Finally, because Sixes resist authority, theories such as the Enneagram make them suspicious and resistant to assessment. One will rarely find a Six in an Enneagram workshop. Sixes need safe places to go. Once they perceive safety, they are able to achieve great things and make wonderful allies. According to Rohr, Sixes are the most common personality type in Western society.[53] The most common vocation for the Six is schoolteacher.

> **The lie Sixes believe:** "It is not okay to trust yourself."
> **The truth Sixes need:** "You are safe."[54]

Type Seven

One word: Enthusiast

Four words: Entertaining, accomplished, uninhibited, manic

Survival strategy: "I must be fun and entertaining."

Sevens exude joy and optimism. They are the men and women at the party who light up the room. Full of idealism and hope, they give the impression that everything is good and beautiful. They are charming and funny, but often carry a childhood wound deep within, which they avoid addressing at all costs through the search for new experiences and endless activity. Appearing to be full of heart, Sevens actually operate from the head. They are strategically motivated. Rohr and Ebert explain:

> Many Sevens have had traumatic experiences, which they did not feel equal to. In order to avoid the repetition of this pain in the future, they have evolved a double strategy: First they repressed or whitewashed their negative and painful experiences. Many Sevens paint their life story in positive colors, even when the scenario was anything but beautiful. . . . Secondly, they've gone into their heads and begun to plan their lives so that every day will promise as much "fun" and as little pain as possible. . . . Sevens would love to live and die at Disneyland.[55]

Sevens are impulsive, responding quickly to personal impulse and desire. They seek adrenaline rushes through change, stimulation, and new experiences. Delayed gratification is the furthest thing from their minds. As a result, Sevens are susceptible to various addictions and chronic anxiety. Riso believes Sevens will choose quantity over quality almost every time.[56] Further, happiness for Sevens is something to be obtained from the outside rather than resourced from within. The next drink, the next party, the next achievement, the next joke, the next relationship—these are the driving motivators for the Seven. Everything needs to scale into bigger, better, and more exciting. Of the fruit of the Spirit listed in Galatians 5:22–23, self-control is the most elusive for the Seven, and joy is ostensibly the most present.

Much of the Seven's activity "is a flight from the painful abysses of their own soul."[57] Because they spend much of their time protecting the image that everything is wonderful, they rarely let anyone too close. Relational commitment and vulnerability are characteristically elusive. It would be too painful, they think, for someone to know their whole story. Pain is to be shifted, not felt. At funerals they move quickly to proclaim how blissful it must be for the deceased to finally be in heaven. Unlike Fours, sitting shiva would be the last thing a Seven would seek after the death of a loved one; Sevens have no clue how to grieve.[58] In fact, grieving means one is doing something wrong in life. Rohr believes these kinds of rationalizations demonstrate Sevens' reliance on cognition as their driving impulse. Similar to Threes, they are in constant danger of ego inflation.[59] And whereas Threes avoid failure, Sevens avoid pain.

Whereas the Six is pessimistic, the Seven is optimistic. Note, however, that optimism is often a strategy for avoiding reality—which can be painful. Sevens aim to avoid emotions when possible. This is why they are more prone to addiction than any other type. Avoidance of pain, discomfort, and ugliness is a central value. They are future-oriented because the future is always bright, which helps them reframe present struggles. Sevens value travel because it can remove present heaviness and does not require any long-term relationship. Experience is another value for Sevens because it can be employed to overcome emptiness. The problem, however, is that once the experience is over, the emptiness returns. Another experience is then required. This partly explains why Sevens, more than any other type, have suicidal tendencies at their most unhealthy. Sevens can reframe any negative into a positive—until they cannot. When they hit this wall, they can become abusive toward others and life-threatening toward themselves.

Underneath their facade, Sevens often feel heavy. They succumb to the pressure to always be the life of the party. Others reinforce this pressure because they seek the Seven to entertain them. Although they make it look effortless, Sevens can experience stress to live up to others' expectations. Rohr claims that where Twos store up love, Sevens store up happiness. The charismatic movement in the contemporary church is full of Sevens, for whom it is Easter all year. Stable, secure, and predictable is a Seven's worst nightmare. Like Fours, Sevens have difficulty with office jobs. However, Sevens can function at an extremely high capacity and have the ability to focus on one thing for a long time—that is, until they get bored and need to move on to the next thing.

> **The lie Sevens believe:** "It is not okay to depend on anyone for anything."
>
> **The truth Sevens need:** "You will be taken care of."[60]

Type Eight

One word: Challenger

Four words: Self-confident, decisive, just, leader

Survival strategy: "I must be strong and in control."

Early in life Eights came to believe that being soft is a disadvantage. Therefore, they compensate with strength, directness, and confrontation. Sometimes their strength is a survival strategy developed in childhood in order to not be taken advantage of or to prove oneself fit for a social group (like a gang member proving their courage to peers). They often take charge of a situation because they fear being under unjust authority. They are ready and willing to fight for the underdog. According to Rohr, outsiders confuse them with Ones because of their aggressive personality. Sex and fighting are both ways for the Eight to connect with others.[61]

Energized by disagreement, Eights see life through a lens of black and white. People are either friends or enemies, and situations are either right or wrong. They are intense.[62] They rarely apologize, and they have difficulty admitting mistakes because of the appearance of weakness.[63] Eights mistrust others until proven otherwise, believing the world to be hostile and threatening. Their disposition toward others is "against." Fortunately, Eights have an acute perception of injustice and are willing, more often than not, to stand against it. They can be great leaders as they intuitively expand themselves to meet whatever need exists in a given moment. Protecting the cause of the weak, Eights are not afraid to use their strength in just causes.[64] Thus, Eights make great leaders of movements. Many attorneys are Eights. However, at times the honesty they demand from others is not first applied to themselves.

Whereas Ones reform a system from within, Eights launch attacks against the system until it changes or collapses. They avoid all perceptions of weakness, helplessness, and subordination. Contrary to expectation, Eights struggle not as much with rage and anger as they do with passion. They are lusty, desirous people who follow their gut instincts. At worst, this means that they tend to exploit others and not respect their dignity. Enjoying retaliation, healthy Eights learn to restrain their strength and channel it into helpful directions. For example, in the civil rights era, Martin Luther King Jr. learned the strength of nonviolence rather than brutal force to effect change.

Unhealthy Eights are accused of controlling others. However, what Eights ultimately seek is to not be under the control of others. A toxic romantic relationship with an Eight often veers into feeling possessed or dominated.

One of the most interesting facets of Eights is how often they are misinterpreted by others. They are more tender than people perceive. Their harsh outer shell belies their soft interior. Few people come to recognize this in Eights because they spend energy hiding what is underneath. Among many reasons for this interpretation is the fact that they speak in imperatives, are impatient with indecision, and struggle when others "beat around the bush."[65] Rarely do Eights notice how others perceive them to be off-putting or aggressive. To them, skirting around the truth is disrespectful. Whereas they seldom bully others, their main competition is themselves.

> **The lie Eights believe:** "It is not okay to trust just anybody."
> **The truth Eights need:** "You will not be betrayed."[66]

Type Nine

One word: Peacemaker
Four words: Peaceful, reassuring, complacent, neglectful
Survival strategy: "I must maintain peace and calm."

Nines often recall childhood memories of feeling overlooked. Over time, they began to believe that the interests and needs of others were more important than their own. They are often interpreted as people who are numb to the world. Twos and Nines look alike. They can easily go with the flow, preferring not to set the pace but rather to assist others along the way. Nines best exude the proverbial question, "Can't we all just get along?" It is said of Nines that they have difficulty distinguishing the tasks that are urgent from those that are not. Thus, they can find themselves with many to-do items but unsure which to tackle first. Palmer avers that as they lose contact with their personal longings because of the importance they place on others' desires, Nines divert energy toward inoculative activities such as watching TV.[67] They lack focus and determination.

Fearing separation from others, Nines do not like to say no. Because they weigh their own opinions as of no more importance than the opinions of others and can easily see all viewpoints as valid, it is easy for them to be persuaded toward another's point of view. A Nine's decision in a conflict can sometimes be no decision. However, they make excellent mediators. Whereas Eights make great attorneys, Nines make great judges because of their ability to see multiple sides of an argument. They are able to express harsh truths in a calm manner, which helps others receive their words.[68] According to Palmer, "Their burden is that they suffer from not knowing what they want, and their blessing is that by having lost a personal position, they are often able to intuitively identify with other people's inner experience. If you identify with each of the Enneagram types, you are very likely a Nine."[69]

Nines like ritual, familiarity, and peace. Appearing humble, Nines are usually insecure and belittle themselves.[70] They are known to struggle with laziness. The upside of that vice is that they are prone to nonviolence. To their detriment, they leave the most important tasks of the day to complete at the end, replacing essential needs with nonessential substitutes.[71] Due to repressed anger, Nines can suffer from inner turmoil and passive aggression. Similar to Twos, Nines have difficulty maintaining a personal position because they are more concerned about whether they agree or disagree with another's viewpoint than about developing their own. People sometimes misinterpret a Nine's silence as tacit agreement when in fact it may simply be indecision. Others report Nines to be on automatic. Although incredibly talented and resourceful for others, Nines can take on a load without letting anything go. Over time, this builds up and can lead to exhaustion or emotional implosion. The young Frodo Baggins from *The Lord of the Rings* is a classic Nine from the onset. Motivating him to save the world from impending evil proves to be a difficult feat—which, ironically, proves him to be a viable candidate due to his lack of interest in authoritarian rule. Along the journey, Frodo moves into an Eight wing (see appendix) and is transformed for the task.

Whereas the Eight needs to be against something, the Nine seeks to avoid conflict altogether. According to Stabile, Nines "have the least energy of all types because they are internally and externally bounded. Believing a personal agenda threatens harmony, they drop their opinion and go along with others."[72] Of all the types, they are the least controlling. They often remain in long relationships; they enjoy nature, are good in ministry positions, and savor the simple pleasures in life.

> The lie Nines believe: "It is not okay to assert yourself."
> The truth Nines need: "Your presence and opinion matters."[73]

practice

Attempt to identify your core type. If you still feel that several are possible, here are some reminder questions that will aid your ability to identify:

1. Which type brings you the greatest amount of humiliation?
2. Can you name your wing? This is helpful if you feel that your core could potentially be one of two types. See the appendix section on wings for more insight.
3. Have you invited a close friend or your partner to help you identify your core type? Only you have access to your motives, but those closest to us can provide excellent feedback.
4. Take an online assessment.[74] Remember that the Enneagram is a motives theory, not a behavior theory. This means that you are often not consciously aware of what drives your behavior. Therefore, assessments can help us narrow the scope but are not reliable methods for identifying one's core type.

Grace is not opposed to effort, but to earning.
—Dallas Willard

Whoever wants to be my disciple must deny themselves and take up their cross and follow me.
—Matthew 16:24

> SKEPTIC'S QUESTION: Discovering my number (En-
> neatype) is the main point of the Enneagram, right?
>
> RESPONSE: No. The Enneagram is a means of self-
> awareness for the purpose of transformation and
> not an end in itself.

F acing a freezing winter morning, a red-hot question began burning inside me. Some thirty community leaders were gathered to spend a day
under the wisdom of Suzanne Stabile. She was teaching
a boutique Enneagram workshop in Greenwich, Con-
necticut, hosted by Ian Morgan Cron. They had not
yet written what would become their wonderful book
The Road Back to You. As she finished her teaching, I
sprinted to the lectern with a searing question: "Who
is writing about the Enneagram as a tool for Christian
discipleship?"

Suzanne paused. She looked down, and then back
at me, musing, "There is nothing I can think of at the
moment."

discipleship spiritual practices for each enneatype

"Are you *kidding* me?" I thought.

I knew my life at that precise moment was about to shift toward a fresh obsession. For the next year, I immersed myself in every book available on the Enneagram, determining to use the theory as a tool toward life transformation for the health of the church and the glory of God. For me the Enneagram is a means for spiritual growth, not an end to reducing ourselves and others to a number. The Enneagram should be seen as a river feeding into a greater body of water, not as a reservoir. It's a thoroughfare, not a cul-de-sac.

The Discipleship Problem

As a pastor, I frequently step back and ask what the local church is meant to be doing. It's easy to get lost in the grind of preaching, planning, and programming. These are necessary tasks within a local church, but tasks alone are incomplete.

I often wonder about the other six days of the week. How are we equipping people for spiritual formation in everyday life? How is the church equipped to *be* the church? Do people have the tools they need to grow on days other than Sunday? Are we helping people discern their uniqueness and how they can most fully step into their God-given callings?

Far too often, for reasons far and wide, the church has sought to "batch" spiritual formation. We tend to treat humans like widgets and assume one size (or in this case, one practice) fits all. The implicit discipleship strategy in many faith communities is fivefold.

1. Show up on Sunday.
2. Read your Bible.
3. Pray.
4. Give.
5. Repeat.

After thirty or so years of Christian discipleship, the hope is that a person will look and act a little more like Jesus. But most people don't feel changed; they just feel older, perhaps a touch more cynical. In the church I was raised in, I was never taught that there are dozens of ways to encounter Scripture, or that maybe my personality is more suited to one particular kind of study than another. I was never taught that there are many ways to pray—that prophetic, contemplative, and intercessory prayer gifts come more naturally (and supernaturally) to some personality types than to others.

Whereas I support each of the five practices above, I do not believe we can take a one-size-fits-all approach to spiritual formation and expect optimal maturity. Enneagram expert Don Richard Riso suggests that there is no single spiritual practice that is right for all people in all places at all times.[1] Churches need to equip people in a variety of spiritual practices because people are diversely motivated.

This is where the Enneagram is incredibly useful, because we can only change what we are able to name. The Enneagram helps us name subconscious patterns that are driving our visible behavior in the world. Once we awaken to those patterns—and the motives that drive them—we can discern specific spiritual practices that will support our growth into maturity.

"Discipleship" is a fancy term for the pathway of submission we choose in order to be spiritually formed into the image of Jesus. This active pursuit takes the form of spiritual practices, which are disciplines that consent to God's slow and patient work in us over time. One must never lose sight that the intent of spiritual practices is always relational connection to God, not the practice itself. When the practice itself becomes the goal, you can be sure that a religious spirit of duty is lurking somewhere nearby (something I will say more about in the next chapter).

Exposure to God's presence through a commitment to spiritual practice, then, is what leads to transformation and ultimately to joining God in the renewal of creation. Moving beyond the Enneagram as a tool to classify people, we use the self-knowledge it imparts and create a personalized spiritual practice as a powerful tool for transforming the ego.

Sandra Maitri reminds us, "The Enneagram is only a map. . . . It will not solve our problems, resolve our issues, or connect us with our depths. It is only information, whose function is to orient and guide us in our inner work, and unless that knowledge is put to use, we do not benefit from it. If it only remains intellectual, it may stimulate our minds and provide interesting diversion and entertainment, but this should not be mistaken for the actual work of transformation. That endeavor is neither rapid nor is it easy."[2]

Since that cold winter morning in 2015, my desire with the Enneagram has been (1) to demystify the theory as the solution to our greatest longings and (2) to use the theory as a way to help people create a personalized spiritual pathway toward deeper transformation. The Enneagram is simply, but profoundly, a method to name our motives—both healthy and unhealthy—in order to choose new habits for ongoing life transformation.

The Discipleship Invitation

Becoming like Jesus cannot happen accidentally. It is always radically intentional. Therefore, discerning specific practices is vital to spiritual growth. Below are two suggestions per Enneatype. These suggestions are not prescriptive, and because everyone has every type within them, many find the practices listed in another type meaningful. Take whatever is helpful.

Each type is assigned two practices—what I refer to as a "downstream" practice and an "upstream" practice. Remember, the Enneagram is like a river serving the greater purpose of life transformation. The downstream practice will come easily to those who identify with a given type, like moving along with the current of a river. This is a good thing and should be continued. The upstream practice, in contrast, will most likely not come easily to those who identify with that particular type. What frequently happens in discipleship is that we do what we are good at and ignore the rest. To use another metaphor: At the gym, I can do bicep curls all day. But you could not pay me enough to sit on the squat machine. Yet if I do only the exercises that come naturally, I will end up with an unbalanced body type. The same principle applies to spiritual disciplines. We need to discern what we veer away from and then face it head-on. Upstream disciplines are critical because these are the practices each type seeks to avoid. In avoiding upstream disciplines, we often evade holistic transformation. And the truth of the matter is that character, maturity, and growth are built in the course of your inner confrontation.[3]

The Enneagram imparts information about where confrontation is most needed. These areas should be explored, not ignored. Riso says, "To climb the levels of development toward integration always requires a struggle against everything that draws us downward."[4] Winemakers testify that the best wine is created only after grapes struggle to compete for the nutrients supplied from the roots. In other words, they must suffer. The taste of good wine derives from struggle and suffering, transformed into something new and enjoyable for others. Likewise, when we experience a kind, loving, and wise person, we can be certain that person has forged their character by facing down inner confrontations.

At the conclusion of each type, a season in the church calendar will be recommended as the most important time of year for your active engagement. (You will also find a more robust list of spiritual practices in the appendix.)

Finally, resist the urge to form a plan at this stage. Simply become aware of the different practices and begin to discern which you are being called to engage in this season. At the conclusion of chapter 6, you will find a guide for creating a rule of life. This is where you will specifically commit to an ongoing rhythm of spiritual discipline.

Type One

The vice of the One is anger, and the One's virtue is serenity. Practices, therefore, should be selected with this trajectory of transformation in mind. Like type Nine, the One also finds nature walks helpful as a downstream practice. Not only does nature rejuvenate a weary soul, but it also lessens the temptation to judge and critique oneself by taking the focus away from the self and shifting it to something grander, wilder, and beyond control. Seeing God in nature can restore a One and calm any brooding anger. Although a One's inner world may not be perfect, God's promise is to perfect all in due time. Nature reminds Ones of God's power, beauty, and capacity to do this.

The upstream discipline for type One is journaling. The trouble with journaling is the honest confession that occurs on paper. To verbally articulate imperfection is difficult, but to record imperfection on paper can be emotionally painful. When we write out the cries of the heart, it can feel more official and somehow truer than if it remains in the head. Therefore, it is easy to understand why journaling would be difficult, particularly for Ones.

However, there is another facet to journaling that provides hope for the One. By recording the details of life (the good, the bad, and the ugly), we gain a sense of the whole. Some refer to this as a kind of "altitude," where distance is created in order to gain perspective. Putting life's complexities into perspective can offer relief to the One, who is prone to feeling overwhelmed. Putting things in writing allows us to review and understand them differently than if they are hidden away in our subconscious or left to weigh on us emotionally and mentally. When journaling, Ones should focus not only on the challenges, imperfections, and tensions of life but also on what is good and what is working in life. Celebration and thanksgiving are key components for the One for ongoing transformation.

The day in the church calendar that Ones should focus on is Good Friday. The Christian tradition observes this as the most painful day in all of human history. On this day, God bore the sin of the world through Jesus's death on the cross. Ones should mark this as the annual reminder that "he was wounded for our transgressions, crushed for our iniquities; upon him was the punishment that made us whole, and by his bruises we are healed" (Isa. 53:5 NRSV). All imperfections were put on Jesus, the perfect one. The Western church tradition includes a liturgical observance of Good Friday called "Tenebrae," which serves as a meaningful way to observe the cross event. At the Tenebrae service, candles are snuffed out after sequential readings of the crucifixion account. After the last candle is extinguished, the congregation leaves in silence, remembering the significance of Jesus's death. Ones are struck by the significance of this service because it reminds them that they do not have to carry their imperfections alone. They can give them to God and trust his eternal plan and his commitment to the process of maturity.

Type Two

Twos must learn to serve *from* love and not *for* love. Thus, receiving love from God must drive a Two's service (rather than receiving love from those being served). Spiritual practices can help with this.

Twos are paradoxes. Whereas they are often the greatest servants, their vice is pride. A healthy and transformed Two will walk in deep humility. Disciplines should be selected with both the vice and virtue in mind. The downstream discipline of the Two is hospitality. Twos know how to bless others. Opening their homes, hearts, and pocketbooks comes easily to them. The key to a transformed Two is serving others as an end and not a means. Healthy Twos serve not out of compulsion but out of conviction. Transformed Twos give because they want to, not because they have to. They also serve and give without any expectations or quid pro quo. Hospitality is a godly ambition when Twos operate from a place of health (Rom. 12:13; 1 Tim. 3:2; Titus 1:8; Heb. 13:2; 1 Pet. 4:9). This can take the form of hosting dinners for guests, serving on mission trips, contributing to local projects, serving in the local church or an organization, or simply being available to others in a time of need. Creating a monthly dinner for friends, acquaintances, or strangers is a helpful rhythm and discipline, especially in a harried and individualistic Western context. Twos should practice hospitality—but without expecting anyone to return the favor.

The upstream practice of the Two is centering prayer. This form of prayer has been used throughout the centuries and has been revitalized in recent decades by Thomas Keating, a Trappist monk in Snowmass, Colorado. Centering prayer is a form of stillness that prioritizes being over doing. It demands that the disciple simply show up before God and surrender any urge for performance, action, or doing. Newcomers to this practice often will connect their breathing with a word. This word stunts the frontal lobe of the brain and helps the person to become still, to listen and sit before God. Solitude can be a struggle with restive Twos because it is like an existential look in the mirror. Centering prayer resides within the apophatic mode of spirituality, meaning that it is accessed through negation or unknowing. The aim in apophatic spirituality is not acquiring information; rather, it is slowing, being, and resting with God. It connotes addition by subtraction, which is a lost pathway in much of the Western church. (To explore more on this pathway, Keating's seminal work *Open Mind, Open Heart* is a helpful resource to begin the journey.)

The day in the church calendar that Twos should most intentionally heed is Maundy Thursday. "Maundy" is derived from the Latin *mandatum*, which means "command." The command Jesus gave during the Last Supper was to love one another. He demonstrated this by washing the disciples' feet. When Peter resisted, Jesus informed him, "Unless I wash you, you have no part with me" (John 13:8). Twos are more comfortable doing the washing than they are receiving it. This day requires that they be served rather than serve. Their vice of pride will cause them to resist. Humility must lead them beyond that temptation and open them to receive the washing.

Type Three

Spiritual disciplines that confront deceit and yield authenticity are valuable for Threes. A preoccupation with image and perception prevents Threes from accessing their true selves. This explains why they often lack self-awareness. The downstream practices for this type can be anything kataphatic, a mode of spirituality that connotes affirmation and acquisition. Practices like Bible study, reading groups, and spiritual courses are helpful for kataphatic learners. For a Three, a 365-day Bible reading plan is beneficial. Naturally, a plan will appeal to the Three's sense of goal orientation and present the opportunity for accomplishment. These kinds of plans inspire this type to achieve a desirable outcome.

The upstream practice that will challenge the Three is confession. Confession requires the disciple to get in touch with what is under the surface. Threes hide from authenticity as a strategy to protect their image in the world. Whereas some church traditions celebrate and offer formal processes of confession, this practice has declined immensely in the last few centuries. This is partly due to a rise in individualism and privatized spirituality. However, one should not neglect the Scripture that implores the church to "confess your sins to each other" (James 5:16). Whether the Three confesses to a priest, a friend, or a group of believers, it is vital that this practice become operative. Confession requires self-examination, emotional connection, and then humble repentance for thoughts and behaviors. As Riso writes, "Change and transformation do not—and cannot—occur without emotional transformation."[5] Although confession is demanding, the practice invites Threes to move from self-deceit to authenticity. From his interpretation of the Philokalia, a collection of teachings from the desert fathers, Anthony Coniaris submits, "To be spiritual is to be in the process of becoming a new creation in Christ."[6] Similar to Ones, Threes have to make peace with the journey, trusting that they do not have to be perfect or project the illusion of competence.

Other recommendations for this type include frequent fasts from social media, which means giving up public displays of success. According to the woes of the Pharisees in Matthew 23, one of the things Jesus despises most is externalism. Threes have to work at ridding themselves of pretense and striving to control the way others perceive them. Essentially, Threes live in the purgatory of meritocracy.

Liturgy comes easy for Threes, but emotional processing and stillness prayer are hard work. Lent is a good season for Threes to practice, but the day in the church calendar that Threes should pay most attention to is Ash Wednesday. This day invokes sobriety that all will die. It calls the church to survey the meaning of pursuits and achievements and then to adjust where there are meaningless pursuits that promote vanity. Transformation is a difficult journey for all, but it is especially difficult for Threes because they must surrender illusion and face reality.

Type Four

Fours wrestle with envy and must strive for emotional balance. Practices should be chosen in view of this pathway to transformation. The downstream practices that come easily to Fours include solitude and journaling. Solitude provides them space to dream, imagine, and think creatively. Without solitude, Fours feel dry. Journaling offers them pages to explore life's meaning and to release the swirl of the inner monologue. Fours enjoy praying through journaling. This type should aim to intercede for others when in solitude and when journaling, as a means of avoiding self-preoccupation. Often, this self-preoccupation can lead to arrogance if life is going well, or to depression if it is not. Exclusive self-focus is what the Four will want to avoid in solitude and journaling.

The upstream practice that Fours need but will aim to avoid is feasting. Feasting should not be viewed only as a time to eat, drink, and be merry but also as a time to bear in mind specific people with whom one can cultivate joy, peace, and thanksgiving. Speaking aloud what one is thankful for opens a community to experiencing joy and celebration. Joy spawns joy. This practice will help the Four get out of himself and also force him away from melancholy. Fours should schedule regular feasting with people they know and trust. Many Fours espouse the need for practices that require structure and for a regimented sleep schedule.

The day in the church calendar that is most important to Fours is Easter. This day is one long celebration that light has come, that death has not overcome despite the darkness of Good Friday. Many Fours can mask their darkness while appearing to be in the light. Easter reminds them that no matter how dark their inner world may be, joy comes in the morning, and there will be a day when that morning light remains forever. These practices and times in the annual cycle will assist the transformation of a Four moving from envy to emotional balance.

Type Five

Fives are in a battle with greed and must move toward non-attachment. Although their greed may be for money, more likely it is greed for knowledge. They seldom share their insight unless asked, and they feel no compulsion to assert their voice. Many Fives are content to hoard their knowledge and do not seek validation from others. They do not realize that what they know can bless others if they would share it. The downstream practice for this type is inductive Bible study. This method of Scripture reading engages the mind while fostering a sense of growth toward God. For example, a word in the original language or an understanding of God's character can deeply move Fives. Reading books on various subject matter is also a helpful practice for the Five.

The upstream discipline for Fives is regular service projects. Fives should aim to get out of their heads and engage their hands. Committing to a consistent mission such as Habitat for Humanity, a soup kitchen, or an after-school program will challenge the Five, who prefers to remain in her head and to acquire information. The Shema, in the Hebrew Bible (Deut. 6:4), reminds the disciple that humans are made to worship God with their whole selves, not just the mind. Engaging the body is necessary for the ongoing transformation of this type. When serving others, Fives are reminded that knowledge can be attained through the hands as well as the head.

The season Fives should pay close attention to is Christmastide. These days are marked as the twelve days of Christmas, during which the church celebrates the arrival of the Messiah. Christmas is a necessary season for them because it brings them back to flesh—to incarnation. The eternal Son of God was enfleshed in a body. Spirituality is both cerebral and carnal. Fives must reject a spiritual-material divide and develop a sacramental imagination that physical matter matters to God. The twelve days of Christmas immerse Christians in this truth.

Type Six

The vice of type Six is fear. Transformative practices will move this type from fear to courage. Singing and journaling are natural practices for this type. Singing reminds Sixes of the truth they can claim. Singing with others solidifies that they are not alone in their convictions. Journaling helps a Six feel safer by allowing them to name the fears of life and reflect on them in writing. It is a way to feel like they have some control or mastery over situations, even if they do not. The downstream practice that Sixes should commit to is a specific way of reading Scripture—*lectio divina* (Latin for "divine reading"). In the sixth century, Benedict of Nursia developed this meditative approach to Scripture reading. The method prioritizes what God is speaking today as much as what God spoke in ages ago. *Lectio divina* invites the Holy Spirit into the reading as it moves the reader in four distinct directions after a text is selected: read, meditate, pray, and contemplate. The benefit of this way of reading Scripture for the Six is to provide a mix of kataphatic and apophatic spirituality. The reader is able to discern Scripture, which builds conviction and courage. Yet this way of Scripture reading also invites the disciple to rest at the end. For a Six who is mired in fear about various facets of life, this practice is essential and natural.

The upstream practice for this type is Scripture memory. To be sure, Scripture memory can feel like an antiquated discipline that most find difficult in a world of sound bites, social media, and overstimulation. Scripture memory can assist the Six in transformation by anchoring him to a commitment to Scripture that goes beyond simply reading. Wherever the Six goes, whatever they face, Scripture has been sown into their soul and can be recalled in times of trouble and anxiety. Ideally, Scriptures should be chosen that remind the person of hope and courage in times of fear and disappointment. For example, when facing a seemingly insurmountable circumstance, recalling Joshua's commission to "be strong and courageous" is meaningful. Furthermore, Scripture memory calls disciples to submit to the authority of Scripture, grounding them in objective reality beyond their circumstances. This can serve as a safe refuge amid confusion and transience.

The season in the church calendar that Sixes should fully embrace is Advent. Advent is the reminder that darkness will not have the final word; the Light is coming. The incarnation teaches the church that fear will never have the last word. Sixes would do well to heed this time of year and live in the tension of the "now" of God's kingdom and the "not yet" of this fallen world. This perspective does not eradicate the possibility of worst-case scenarios coming true, but it does provide hope that whatever transpires is within God's sovereign purpose and that he will work together all things for good.

Type Seven

The transformation of Sevens is the invitation to move from gluttony to sobriety. In the twenty-first century, the term "gluttony" is linked with the problem of obesity in the United States and other wealthy Western countries. Overeating is certainly a form of gluttony, but the problem extends beyond the waistline. Excess has become a Western value. Americans "supersize" everything from burgers and alcohol to credit cards and entertainment. We spend an entire weekend "binge watching" television shows. Sevens are particularly prone to excess in various areas of life. Practices should be selected with this in mind. The recommended downstream practice of the Seven is feasting. Many Sevens are gregarious, extroverted, and exciting to be around. They feed off energy and seldom shy away from standing at the center of a moment. Feasting gives them reason to enjoy life with others. When Sevens practice feasting they should connect it with purpose, such as having meaningful conversations that develop relationships or praying alongside others. When they feast, this type should keep in mind the propensity of excess and seek to ensure they do not overindulge in any way. They must also remember that Scripture calls the body the temple of the Holy Spirit (1 Cor. 6:19). Second, Sevens must not exploit feasting to avoid their inner life. Cultivating a robust inner life yields greater meaning when feasting with others. When a Seven ceases to pursue others while feasting and merely seeks attention for her- or himself, it might be a clue that self-love is at the center.

The upstream practice for this type is solitude and silence for a specified period of time each day. Sevens must discipline their lives to look within. Solitude releases them from performance for others. Silence reminds them of the quiet whisper of the Spirit within, which serves to counsel, convict, and intercede (Rom. 8:26–27). Sevens should set aside time each day for solitude and silence. Mornings, before the rush of the day begins, are a good time for this. This sacred time serves as a reminder to Sevens that their identity is not based on how others feel about them, nor is it based on how they feel about themselves. Rather, it is grounded in God's pronouncement of their belovedness, which the practice of silence and solitude allows them to recall and live from for the rest of the day.

The time in the church calendar this type should most intentionally heed is Lent. Lent is a forty-day period of self-reflection, sobriety, and self-control. Beginning with Ash Wednesday, Lent reminds followers of Jesus that they will die and are living in a spiritual battle. Just as Jesus went into the desert for forty days before beginning his public ministry, so Christians are called to follow Jesus into the desert of their inner lives, to discern where growth is most urgent. During this season, another practice that is both helpful and challenging to Sevens is fasting. Fasting instills dependency on God for all things, reminding followers of their true longings. Jesus once said that man does not live by bread alone but by the words that come from God's mouth (Matt. 4:4). Fasting invites the disciple to say "no" to good things in order to say "yes" to the best thing.

Type Eight

Eights are justice-oriented. The downstream practice for this type is to commit to regular opportunities to contend for the common good. This can take various paths such as serving weekly in a local soup kitchen, advancing a cause that is worthwhile, or raising funds for those who are deprived of necessities such as water or medical supplies. Eights naturally come to the rescue of others and are not afraid to get involved. Although they are sometimes perceived as aggressive, healthy Eights are aggressive toward causes they most believe in.

The upstream discipline Eights need is accountability among those whom they trust. This type avoids vulnerability. They are often unaware of how others perceive them. For an Eight to move toward holistic transformation, they must invite others to provide feedback about their life and conduct. Connecting with a small group in the local church or regularly pursuing open conversation with trusted friends must be intentionally sought, or else it is unlikely to ever occur. Because Eights can be intimidating, others will find it difficult to provide the feedback they most need. This puts the onus of responsibility on the Eight to seek out others, invite their honesty, and humbly receive their feedback. The writer of Proverbs says, "Wounds from a friend can be trusted" (27:6). Trusted friends are able to love in truth. Trusted friends smooth out our jagged edges.

The season in the church calendar that Eights should most intentionally engage is Pentecost, which serves to remind them that God cares about justice even more than they do. The Scriptures purport that God is making all things new (Rev. 21:5). Partnering with God relieves the heavy load of individually carrying justice in the world. This posture can also instruct Eights to value justice without demonizing opponents. Believing God will have the final word in every situation can assist this type in fighting for justice, submitting to God, and resting in the truth that, in time, all will be put to rights. As Eights engage the world with the hope of justice, their prayer becomes, "Come, Lord Jesus."

Type Nine

Whereas the vice of the Nine is sloth, the virtue is action. Therefore, it is helpful to think of transformation for the Nine in terms of engagement and conviction. The downstream practice that will come easy for the Nine is spending time in creation. Whether walking, hiking, climbing, strolling along the beach, or running in a park, these activities will aid the Nine in restoring balance. Spending time in nature also serves as a calming practice in the midst of the details of life for a Nine, offering rest and an opportunity to return to life with a restored sense of peace and calm. Nines are often in the middle of conflict, operating as intermediaries between conflicted parties; they need nature's regular reminders that life does have order despite its complexities.

The upstream practice for this type is fixed-hour prayer. Jesus entered a Jewish context where the community oriented its life around three specific times of prayer—morning, noon, and evening. The early Christians followed the formation of the Didache, a formation manual that prescribed prayer three times each day.[7] Since that time, many variations of fixed-hour prayer have emerged. Trappists are perhaps the community most rigorously oriented around prayer. This monastic order even rises throughout the night to pray. Fixed-hour prayer, often referred to as the "Liturgy of the Hours," can be helpful to a Nine because it prioritizes God's presence and the practice of seeking God's wisdom and guidance amid the hustle and hurry of life. Rising and praying throughout the night may not be for everyone, but stopping three times per day—upon waking, before lunch, and prior to bed are three natural times—to recenter oneself toward God is well within reach for all of us, including Nines. Benedictines, whose monastic order was founded by Benedict of Nursia in Monte Cassino, Italy, refer to the three times of prayer as *lauds* (morning prayer), *diurnum* (noon prayer), and *compline* (night prayer). The priority of prayer is challenging to Nines, who sometimes find themselves confused about what matters most within a calendar full of activities and responsibilities. It may also be helpful for this type to meet regularly with a spiritual director who can assist them in discerning life decisions.

The church calendar season that Nines should heed is Epiphany. Beginning with the arrival of the Magi at the manger of Jesus, Epiphany reminds the church of her vocation to face outward toward the other, to share the light of Christ. This season in the calendar challenges Nines to be bold in using their voice. Nines are rarely in danger of overexerting or overvocalizing, so this prescription for boldness can prove instructive and formational, challenging Nines not to allow their longing for peace and restoration (or their desire to avoid conflict) to keep them silent. Lasting peace and restoration have been made available through the cross and resurrection of Christ. Sharing this good news with others is the meaning of Epiphany, and it is good medicine, especially for the Nine.

What you are thinking every moment of every day becomes a physical reality in your brain and body.
—Caroline Leaf

These commandments that I give you today are to be on your hearts. Impress them on your children. Talk about them when you sit at home and when you walk along the road, when you lie down and when you get up. Tie them as symbols on your hands and bind them on your foreheads. Write them on the doorframes of your houses and on your gates.
—Deuteronomy 6:6–9

SKEPTIC'S QUESTION: Can we actually know the Enneatype of biblical figures?

RESPONSE: Due to limited information, not really. However, the point of this chapter is not to reduce biblical figures to a type but to help us see how we play out the same default patterns in our present context. Perhaps the Scriptures are far more relevant than we previously believed.

T he colors are endless. From Indian fig trees to exotic orchids, the reddest of roses to irises of every purple hue. Imagine 158 acres of natural, curated beauty teeming from the ground. This magical place is real, located on the east side of Grand Rapids,

scripture finding your type in the biblical narrative

Michigan. Meijer Gardens is essentially a theme park for flowers. Nestled in the many gardens one will find sculptures that draw on engaging themes. These sculptures have been sourced from all over the world, from the legendary works of Auguste Rodin to the recent provocative pieces of Ai Weiwei. Although the gardens seem to be one of West Michigan's best-kept secrets, they are a spectacle to behold and one of my greatest boasts about living in Grand Rapids.

Over the years, one sculpture in particular has moved me. Artist Bill Woodrow calls this piece *Listening to History*.[1] Although probably not the artist's intent, I cannot help seeing how Woodrow's sculpture captures the role the Scriptures play in

Photo taken by AJ Sherrill with permission of both the artist and Frederik Meijer Gardens

Listening to History by Bill Woodrow

the Christian's life. When we close our eyes to the surrounding cultural scripts, the Bible defines reality and dictates how one should navigate the epic journey toward Christlikeness.

Reclaiming the "Script" in "Scripture"

The obvious root of the word "Scripture" is "script." The Bible intends to script—or "story"—us amid surrounding cultural scripts that are vying for our allegiance and affection. Today's cultural scripts are most often oriented around what you purchase, who you vote for, or which ideological, ethnic, or regional group you identify with. The Bible, therefore, aims both to prevent us from making these lesser cultural stories our dominant stories and instead make God's story of redemption the center of our lives.

At the risk of controversy, I believe the central purpose of Scripture is not first to indoctrinate with theological propositions meant simply to reside in our heads. Rather, the Bible's central purpose is to invite us to participate in the unfolding of God's drama in the world. And this drama is one in which the triune God is redemptively at work in everyone, everywhere. This is the story that has been unfolding since the dawn of time.

But here is the problem: it is quite possible that since Gutenberg's invention of the printing press, the world has never had more Bibles printed and fewer Bibles read. Ben Irwin, a creator of the *Community Bible Experience*, rightly notes the vast difference between "best-selling" and "most-read."[2] In the West, biblical literacy seems to be at an all-time low. In the average Christian home, the Bible often serves as a kind of artifact, a dusty relic of the past that rests on a shelf low enough to be noticed yet high enough to go untouched. It is obvious, then, why the dominant lens through which many Christians in the West see themselves today is not the biblical script but instead the competing cultural scripts.

By and large, emerging generations of churchgoers cannot recall many of the stories that have been handed down to us from the Prophets, the Gospels, and the Epistles. Few today profess to have been adequately "storied." It is no wonder why many young people renounce Christian faith; to them, the story of Scripture just doesn't seem compelling enough to compete against the scripts doled out by advertisers, filmmakers, and other cultural creators. These scripts are not all bad, but rarely do they tell the story that God is writing.

In the Judeo-Christian faith (and the Muslim faith, for that matter), we believe that we are dealing with a God who has determined to speak. At times God's speech pours through creation (Gen. 1; Rom. 1:20), at times God's speech pours through prophets (Heb. 1:1), and in a unique generation God's speech was enfleshed (John 1:14; Heb. 1:2). At other times God's speech was written down (2 Tim. 3:16; Rev. 1:11). The speech that was written down and is universally applicable is referred to as Scripture. Through the centuries there has been some debate as to what does and does not qualify as Scripture. But, miraculously, there is significant agreement about the sixty-six books that are compiled in the Scriptures today.

Yet today many Christians face obstacles to seeing Scripture afresh. Too many misperceive the Bible as an irrelevant artifact or as chock-full of banal history lessons—or worse, as oppressive dogma from a previous era. Each of these overgeneralizations leads us away from the central meaning of the sacred text. The purpose of the Scripture is to step into the story God is still writing. The Scriptures tell a unified narrative in four themes: creation, fall, redemption, and renewal. We are meant to see ourselves in the people who have come before us.

This is where the Enneagram can be quite useful as a tool to bring us back into the Bible. Each section below attempts to make connections between your personality and the personalities of the people of God who have come before you. While we cannot say we know with certainty the Enneatypes of the people in Scripture, we can nonetheless draw type themes from the different scriptural narratives.

In some narratives, you will find your type triumphing over the fall. In others, you will see how unhealth led to disarray and death. The stories of the Bible are (among many things) archetypes of how humans continue in the same patterns of behavior, generation after generation.[3] The aim is to find yourself, through other biblical figures, in the drama of Scripture. For example, whether you subscribe to original sin is beside the point. What is clear is that my tendency to distrust God and act on my own authority is the same temptation Adam and Eve faced in the garden account. I can easily find myself in their moment of temptation. Like them, I eat from the fruit of autonomy almost daily. Like them, I experience shame and self-condemnation. And like them, I must be regularly restored to fellowship with a loving God.

The story of Scripture is the story we inhabit every day. Their world is our world. Although the political and cultural makeup of the ancient Near East is obviously different from our own, the themes of human behavior are constant. In the book *Biblical Characters and the Enneagram*, authors Diane Tolomeo, Pearl Gervais, and Remi De Roo conclude, "The stories of scripture appeal to our understanding and experience of human beings in diverse emotional states at the same time that they speak to us about ourselves and our inner life. If we see Abraham and Sarah, Moses and Mary, Deborah and Martha, not solely as figures in biblical history but also as representing aspects of ourselves, we begin to understand their stories as intimately connected with our own stories, and they can become mentors in teaching us about our inner lives."[4]

To live into wisdom is to learn from those who have come before us. The goal of this chapter is to reconnect the ancient texts with contemporary life so that you may be re-storied into the drama of God and may find yourself connected to streams that expand far beyond your lifetime.

Scripture Identification

Type One

One word: Perfectionist

Core narrative: Apostle Paul (Acts 8–28 and Paul's Epistles)

Memory passage: Matthew 19:26

The big picture for Ones is this: Learn to embrace grace as a gift and not a problem. Ones tend to emphasize idealistic and perfectionistic tendencies. The biblical narrative Ones may most identify with is that of the apostle Paul. Consider the way Paul defends his credibility to the Philippian Christians. Apparently, legalism had crept back into the community from false teachers. Paul details his résumé: "If anyone else has reason to be confident in the flesh, I have more: circumcised on the eighth day, a member of the people of Israel, of the tribe of Benjamin, a Hebrew born of Hebrews; as to the law, a Pharisee; as to zeal, a persecutor of the church; as to righteousness under the law, blameless" (Phil. 3:4–6 NRSV). Paul had skillfully and meticulously honed his list of achievements before encountering a theophany on the road to Damascus.

Sometimes the greatest blessing for Ones is to be "knocked off their horse." In the next section of his letter to the Philippians, Paul writes that he considers all of his former accomplishments nothing compared to what he received in Christ through faith. At first glance, one may conclude that Paul was a healthy Three in this passage, particularly since Threes are prone to highlight their achievements as identity banners. Certainly there are achiever tendencies in Paul's past, but he relates to the One because of his propensity to anger as a vice. Another reason to identify Paul with the One type is related to the *quality* of his achievements: for example, "as to righteousness under the law, blameless." For a Three, the achievement of simply being a Pharisee would be sufficient. But for a One, perfection within that achievement is paramount. Threes are efficient, so the title Pharisee is enough. Ones are perfectionistic, so being the best Pharisee of all matters most.

Recall that Ones are also known as reformers. Paul literally killed Jews who followed Jesus. Formerly Saul, an ancient religious bounty hunter, upon conversion he received the name Paul, meaning "little one." Ones want to believe they are always right. For Saul to receive the name Paul was nothing short of a transformed personality. He had spent his entire life perfecting his résumé, but in an instant it became rubbish to him as he began a new vocation of transforming his anger into love. This is the reason he emphasizes *metanoia* ("repentance" in Greek) throughout his works. Imagine a One who has journeyed so far down one path, only to have to turn around and head the opposite direction. This takes maturity; this is repentance.

Unhealthy Ones would often rather be wrong and committed to one path than be right and have to turn around. When Ones realize the error of their ways, it can paralyze them in self-pity and deep regret.[5] Healthy Ones can detach themselves from anger and perfection, admit their flaws, and seek restoration. This is Paul's narrative in a nutshell. Moreover, healthy Ones can draw on errors of the past to assist others in avoiding pitfalls, which is Paul's writing tactic in Philippians 3.

According to Tolomeo, Gervais, and De Roo, "The more Paul 'gains Christ,' the more his ego is liberated (Phil. 3:8–9)."[6] Other Scriptures provide typing insight into Paul. After his conversion, he still tends toward self-righteousness and inflexibility at times. This explains some of the aggressive tone in his letters, particularly when he confronts Peter and on another occasion parts ways with Barnabas, his former mentor and companion, over a ministerial difference that was nondoctrinal (Acts 15). In the letter to the Galatians, Paul wishes that those who unsettle Christians back into legalism "would castrate themselves" (5:12

NRSV). Inflexibility in Ones toward others can cause great relational rupture. Yet it is the self-rigidity and self-perfection that can be most crushing when headed in an unhealthy direction within personality. Paul writes to the community in Rome of his inner conflict: "For I do not do what I want, but I do the very thing I hate. . . . For I know that nothing good dwells within [my flesh]" (Rom. 7:15, 18 NRSV). An unhealthy Paul would tend toward self-hate and chronic shame. However, healthy Ones are able to repent of sin and imperfection of every kind, offer their shortcomings to God, and receive restoration through divine grace.

The New Testament passage on which Ones should focus, ironically, comes from the Sermon on the Mount: "Be perfect, therefore, as your heavenly Father is perfect" (Matt. 5:48). The ostensible curse of this text is the attempt to live up to a standard impossible through the flesh. This is what Paul condemns time and again after conversion. However, Jesus's teaching reminds the reader that perfection is a noble, God-ordained pursuit. Like Paul, it is attainable *through repentance and grace*. Without cooperation with the Spirit of God, it is impossible. As Matthew later records, Jesus taught that "for mortals it is impossible, but for God all things are possible" (19:26 NRSV).

Therefore, for the One, repentance is the supreme gift of God. Repentance is a cause for joy, not despair. Ones would do well to focus on repentance as a way toward being perfected in this life.

Type Two

One word: Helper

Core narrative: Parable of the sheep and the goats (Matthew 25:31–46)

Memory passage: Matthew 7:11

The big picture for the Two is this: Before you do anything, check your motives. Twos value feelings and long to be loved, which, for an unhealthy Two, is what motivates them to offer love in the form of service to others. Reciprocity is often a value of the Two: if they give love, they expect love in return. One can see, then, why pride is a challenging vice for this type. Twos face four preeminent issues: seeking unconditional love, fearing interpersonal rejection, searching for intimacy, and needing to nurture others to feel valuable.[7]

The biblical account that best captures the essence of the Two is the parable of the sheep and the goats (Matt. 25:31–46). Although parables are not historical accounts, they are equally true, for they aid in identifying the reader within the text and suggest a pathway toward transformation and wholeness. This particular parable is eschatological. Christ returns and begins to divide the nations. Jesus likens one group to sheep and the other to goats. When all is complete, the ones at his right hand are invited to partake in the fullness of the eternal kingdom; the ones on his left are commanded to depart from his presence and enter eternal punishment. This is one of the strongest, most direct parables that Jesus teaches. The difference between the sheep and the goats is acts of service. The sheep, who are on the right, are praised for the way they cared for those who are poor, oppressed, and downtrodden. During their lives, they fed the hungry, gave drink to the thirsty, clothed the naked, and visited the sick and those in prison (vv. 35–36). The astounding revelation of the parable is how closely Jesus identifies with the poor, the oppressed, and the downtrodden. In fact, he sees himself as one of them—when these people are taken care of, Jesus himself is cared for. The implication of the text is that Jesus so cares for the poor that a deed done to them is the same as a deed done to him. Within the greater Roman world, this kind of identification would have been rare at best and most likely unheard of.

Conversely, those sorted to the left are likened to goats who neglected the poor, the broken, and the downtrodden. They claim to have not seen Jesus as sick, poor, or hungry, so they wonder how they could possibly have neglected him—a fair defense for those who do not know just how deeply Jesus identifies with the downtrodden. According to Tolomeo, Gervais, and De Roo, the group on his right "simply did what needed to be done, with no awareness of being unusually good or giving, or the reward of going home with the glow of having done an act of charity. It was just something that happened: done and forgotten."[8] Neither those to his left nor those to his right understood how closely Jesus identifies with the poor.

Nevertheless, it is revealed that Jesus rewards those who love the person in front of them who is in need—to love that person is to love Christ himself. The lesson through this parable is paramount to the Two because of the "quality of unattachment."[9] The sheep are not even aware of their action. They performed the action with no expectation in return. This kind of love represents what biblical scholar John Barclay calls "incongruous grace."[10]

Twos want to be loved, which is the motivating factor for giving love. By contrast, Jesus is pleased with those who give love, expecting nothing in return. Scripture invites Christians to love because they have already been loved beyond measure. In John's first epistle they love because he first loved (1 John 4:19). Healthy Twos recognize the presence of grace and love in the first place.

For the Christian who is a Two, the task is to solidify her identity in Christ by grace and then recall her identity through spiritual practices before moving into the tasks of the day. These practices will aid Twos in demonstrating love as an extension of God's love into the world, rather than expecting reciprocity when performing an act of service. The following chapter will detail specific, helpful practices for this type. When Twos perform an act of service, they pause and reflect before helping to ensure proper motives. For example, Jesus teaches that when giving charity, "do not let your left hand know what your right hand is doing" (Matt. 6:3). Well aware of humans' propensity to manipulate and self-deceive, Jesus instructs his followers to practice righteousness in secret so that their motives remain pure and solely unto God.

The core passage Twos should know as they move toward health is Matthew 7:11: "If you then, who are evil, know how to give good gifts to your children, how much more will your Father in heaven give good things to those who ask him!" (NRSV). Where this passage best connects with and instructs Twos is in the fact that God, the Father, is both aware of and satisfies one's needs. Once this type recognizes God's gift and receives it, there are ample resources to be generous and helpful toward others without needing reciprocity to feel whole. God is love, and God gives love freely through the gift of the indwelling Spirit of Christ. (To see how this works out in relationship, see the account of Ruth and Boaz from the book of Ruth in the Hebrew Scriptures.) Of all nine types, Twos most need to apprehend the height, depth, and grandeur of the grace God has lavished on those who love him and are called according to his purposes.

Type Three

One word: Achiever
Core narrative: King Saul (1 Samuel 8–15)
Memory passage: 1 Corinthians 13:1

The big picture for Threes is this: your greatest gift can become your greatest curse. Unhealthy Threes live from the feelings of controlling others' perception of them. Image is their primary vice. They therefore have difficulty accessing their own feelings. Because success (or the perception of success) is of utmost importance to Threes, mature inner qualities and self-awareness can remain elusive. Often their relationships give the appearance of being genuine, but they can remain entirely superficial without the Three's knowledge or awareness. Unlike Ones, who seek to be perfect, Threes desire to appear perfect in their many endeavors. Ambition, ability to motivate, and the craving for success drive Threes in decision-making.[11] For these reasons, the rise and downfall of King Saul is a helpful narrative for this type.

The narratives of King Saul and King David reveal Three characteristics. Here, we will focus on Saul. From the onset, neither was born into royalty, but both were raised in rural obscurity. Saul was anointed as the first king of Israel. Before his time, the nation was ruled by a series of judges. The people cried out to God to make them like other nations, to give them a king who would rule over them. God gave them what they asked in the form of Saul. The text of 1 Samuel 8 makes clear that Saul was handsome—something that is often extremely important to a Three. First Samuel 9:2 reads, "There was not a man among the people of Israel more handsome than he; he stood head and shoulders above everyone else" (NRSV). Society looks to leaders who carry the *physical* appearance of success, especially in the contemporary world of visual media.

When reading 1 Samuel 8–12, one is struck by Saul's good nature. He does not appear to clamor for image and success. In fact, rather than asserting his own preeminence, Saul is sought out by Samuel, who comes to anoint him king. In his early life, Saul appears to be in touch with his feeling center. In fact, when searching for missing donkeys (9:5), he returns home because he senses his father may grieve his absence and begin to worry.

This is a cue that Saul is aware of how others feel. Some Enneagram experts surmise that Threes often aim to make the family proud from a young age. When Samuel approaches Saul about the prospect of becoming king, Saul is genuinely surprised. His humility is obvious from 1 Samuel 9:21. One of the turning points in Saul's life comes when he is filled with the spirit of God and turned into a different person (10:6). This transformative act of God, growing Saul into a powerful king, later works against Saul as ambition and entitlement cause him to seize more power and become jealous. He begins to identify more with the person he becomes than with the humble heritage from which he came. It is important for Threes to remain grounded in their past and in real relationships in the present that speak truthfully. Otherwise, self-preoccupation can take a Three down—and eventually, down Saul went.

A definitive turning point in Saul's character takes place two years into his reign, while Samuel is transitioning out of his prophetic role alongside Saul. Accountable relationships are vital for a Three. Once Samuel steps out, everything changes. Due to Saul's early military success and the absence of accountability, he learns to rely on his achievements rather than on God's word. First Samuel 13 records an account that displays Saul's commitment to success over obedience. The Philistines are mounting an attack against Israel, and Samuel is delayed. Saul decides to take the priestly matters into his own hands. The account is thus:

> [Saul] waited for seven days, the time appointed by Samuel; but Samuel did not come to Gilgal, and the people began to slip away from Saul. So Saul said, "Bring the burnt offering here to me, and the offerings of well-being." And he offered the burnt offering. As soon as he had finished offering the burnt offering, Samuel arrived; and Saul went out to meet him and salute him. Samuel said, "What have you done?" Saul replied, "When I saw that the people were slipping away from me, and that you did not come within the days appointed, and that the Philistines were mustering at Michmash, I said, 'Now the Philistines will come down upon me at Gilgal, and I have not entreated the favor of the LORD'; so I forced myself, and offered the burnt offering." Samuel said to Saul, "You have done foolishly; you

have not kept the commandment of the LORD your God, which he commanded you. The LORD would have established your kingdom over Israel forever, but now your kingdom will not continue; the LORD has sought out a man after his own heart; and the LORD has appointed him to be ruler over his people, because you have not kept what the LORD commanded you." (vv. 8–14 NRSV)

Threes are so determined to succeed that they take matters into their own hands, often making the original dilemma worse. Efficiency is a significant vice for the Three and can lead to impatience and self-assertion. For this reason, unhealthy Threes are frustrated in a team dynamic. For Saul, matters only spiral downward. Rather than seeking humility, accountability, and repentance, Saul's heart hardens into self-protection, fear, and jealousy. This is most evident when young David, a shepherd in rural obscurity, slays the giant Philistine that Saul could not. Saul's jealousy later grows to rage as the people of Israel honor David more than Saul. It ends with Saul chasing David down to end his life. David is Saul's mirror image. Both are Threes, but David learns to face his downfalls (see the narrative of David, Bathsheba, and Uriah in 2 Sam. 11–12) and repent. Saul, on the other hand, never matures, as one cover-up leads perpetually to another, resulting in a man who will always be remembered as the treacherous first king of Israel.

The Scripture passage that Threes should commit to mind and heart is 1 Corinthians 13:1: "If I speak in the tongues of men or of angels, but do not have love, I am only a resounding gong or a clanging cymbal." It does not matter what one achieves or fails in; what matters is whether the underlying motive is love or self-exaltation. Love leads one to greater measures of humility, grace, and compassion. Self-exaltation is a downward spiral leading to coercion, jealousy, and pride. No matter how ostensibly generous or gifted one may appear, when ambition or achievement is the primary goal, love is never present. This is unacceptable for the people of God.

> ### Type Four
>
> **One word:** Individualist
>
> **Core narrative:** Job
>
> **Memory passage:** Deuteronomy 6:4

The big picture for Fours is this: your feelings about your circumstances do not define your identity, nor do they capture the whole of reality. As feelers, Fours naturally retreat within themselves and are known for their radical individualism. This often leads to them feeling a certain uniqueness about themselves that separates them from the world. Enneagram expert A. H. Almaas writes, "Uniqueness is not specialness; all unique beings are expressions of the same divine Source."[12] The Shema (Deut. 6:4) is very important for the Four to grasp as he moves toward maturity. Central to faith for both Christians and Jews is to love God and others. Further, it is to recognize that God is one. To be in God is not only to recognize his uniqueness—which Ones do so well—but also to notice his interconnectedness with others, just as God is interconnected in Trinity. As Don Richard Riso and Russ Hudson suggest in their work *The Wisdom of the Enneagram*, the more self-focused and disconnected from others a person becomes, the more ardently his personality type can attach to ego as identity.[13] Connectedness is often a missing element in the Four's life that leads to immaturity and, at worst, self-harm. For this reason, the biblical narrative to which Fours should pay attention is the rise, fall, and triumph of Job.

Job's narrative is about spiritual maturity, moving from an individualist mindset to a cosmic hope. Preoccupied by what he once had and then lost, Job is driven to the precipice of despair. Essentially, this narrative illustrates how to view God (and humanity) when life does not go as planned. It is a narrative of self-understanding. The reader should not become overly preoccupied as to whether this account happened in a specific time and place but should pay attention to *how* this account happens. Theodicy is one of the greatest challenges to speak hope into within a world riddled with terrorism, decay, and sickness. It must be asked: What does the presence of these enemies mean about the nature of God?

Job is a Four in the sense that he spends a significant amount of time analyzing his feelings. Job's small world has collapsed and disappeared in a matter of days. Although the loss of children, material goods, and one's own health is indeed tragic, the reader is left internalizing questions about what all this means: Can God be praised in despair? Is anyone entitled to what Americans have called "the good life"? Is life itself something we are entitled to, or is it a gift? According to Tolomeo, Gervais, and De Roo,

> What [Job] has to learn is that speaking tragically or dramatically is part of a self-image that needs to be destroyed. It comes from a belief that things should be a certain way, namely, the way we want them to be. When things do not cooperate with what we want, we take it personally and feel that the universe is against us. . . .
>
> After all has been suffered, can we accept the innate being of things as they are and not expect to receive any tangible reward, and even leave ourselves relaxed and open to the experience of pain and sorrow?[14]

The transformative issue for Job is not grieving what has been lost; rather, it is identifying so deeply with what was lost, which was only ever meant to be enjoyed. Ash Wednesday speaks precisely into this narrative by reminding disciples that they come from dust and to dust they shall return. Nothing is permanent.

All will die. Possessions do not last. Unhealthy Fours take this to mean that life is wholly tragic and, therefore, not worth living. Healthy Fours can recognize the transience of this reality and enjoy life as a gift while it lasts. Fours have a transformative decision to make: Is life tragedy or comedy, or can we simply say "it is what it is" in every season?

Fours tend to withdraw when life takes a circumstantial downturn. Tolomeo, Gervais, and De Roo assert, "Religious joy arises from knowing there is nothing we can do or know about anything compared to the vastness of God. Our response can be to see life therefore as tragic, or to plunge through its suffering and find equanimity. . . . Job, however, does not regard his life as anything but tragic. His resignation is not life-giving but imprisoning for him, focusing on his calamity and loss."[15] Job's temptation, over and against his wife's advice, is not to curse God but to curse his own life (3:1). Ultimately, the hard work for the Four is to remember that life is a gift to receive.

Because the gift of life is fleeting, a Four cannot cling to what she has as her identity. Transformation lies not only in accessing this perspective but also in inviting others along on the journey, in being able to laugh together and mourn together, whatever the season. When in despair, the Four will not find answers by retreating into a state of woe. One must recall that envy is the core vice for the Four. At the beginning of the account, Job lives an envious and enviable life. His friends see it, and so does the Accuser (Satan), but Job doesn't. Fours struggle to see the envy others have of them and are preoccupied with envying what they themselves feel they lack. Implied in Satan's accusations is the question, "Why Job?" Perhaps even his friends wondered, in reflecting on Job's great wealth, "Why not us? Why him?"

How rare it is, though, for us to ask, *when things are good*, "Why me?" For Fours in particular, the difficulty and infrequency of this kind of self-reflection reveals their expectations and entitlements toward life, rather than their sense of receiving all things as gifts and being willing to let them go since they are inferior to identity. The narrative of Job is about moving beyond individual pleasure, rewards, and blessing and moving into experiencing a cosmic deity who is the center of creation. When one begins to do this, lament can take an appropriate place in loss rather than disrupting core identity. This is precisely what occurs when God answers Job with a series of rhetorical questions.

Type Five

One word: Investigator

Core narrative: Nicodemus (John 3, 7, 19)

Memory passage: Hebrews 11:32–40

Here is the big picture for Fives: you must learn to integrate your mind into your heart and your body. As thinkers, Fives naturally research, observe, and investigate. They seek to know everything concerning what they are immersed in, and they can devote themselves to one single task at a time. Einstein once wrote that the sole thing he wanted to know was the mind of God: all the rest was just details.[16]

Unhealthy Fives fear incompetence and often possess a greed for knowledge that they hoard for themselves. As a result, Fives may find themselves withdrawn, isolated, and lonely. Since what they know in their heads often remains detached from emotions (heart) and will (hands), they seek independence from anything that would demand something from them. This manifests as running from relationships where their autonomy could be threatened or could be as simple as an unwillingness to use their gifts in community. Their quest for autonomy spawns disconnection from others. Healthy Fives have learned the imperative of interconnected living and often bless others with their wealth of knowledge and insight. Nicodemus, from John's Gospel, displays Five tendencies as he wrestles with truth and the implications of Jesus's teachings if integrated into the whole of his life. The reader can view his growth in spiritual maturity as the Gospel unfolds. As the Scriptures reveal, in conversion to the way of Jesus, Nicodemus loses his status as a Pharisee and joins a new community of disciples because of the integration of his convictions into his everyday life.[17]

The process of Nicodemus's conversion narrative—via investigation—is notable in John 3, 7, and 19. It is a process that begins "at night," in the dark (3:2), as he furtively seeks to inquire about the messiahship of Jesus, "the light" (1:4). Nicodemus is a seminal example of type Five moving from unhealth to health. He is transformed by the renewing of his mind (Rom. 12:2). However, Nicodemus has to learn on his journey that in order to be fully transformed, he must engage not only his mind but also his heart and even his body in willful action. The Engel scale—a discipleship evaluation assessment developed by James Engel—provides a helpful perspective of the stages a type Five undergoes to arrive at bearing witness to Christ in the public square. Additionally, Eastern Orthodox Christians might describe Nicodemus's conversion process using the categories of illumination, purgation, and union.[18] Fives must be permitted three essential ingredients for transformation to occur: information, time, and safety. Jesus provides each of these for Nicodemus.

We first encounter Nicodemus in John 3. He is a Pharisee, which means he has advanced knowledge in the Torah. He is also curious about Jesus—so curious that he comes to Jesus in the night, implying that he came in secret. Unhealthy Fives avoid risk at all costs. They keep information stored in their minds and refuse to release it until all mysteries and questions are solved. Nicodemus needs more information from Jesus before following him. When Jesus calls the initial twelve disciples, he does not give them a treatise about his authenticity, nor does he set up a question-and-answer session to alleviate their fears. Instead, he works a few wonders to support his legitimacy and then invites them to follow him. This strategy does not work with Fives, and it certainly did not work with Nicodemus. The invitation of Jesus into discipleship involves one's body and not mere cognitive assent. Fives are often out of touch with their bodies, preferring to remain in their heads. Nicodemus does not leave his time with Jesus converted. Fives seek rational, reasonable, systematic categories of truth. Jesus frequently taught in parables, metaphors, and paradoxes. To Jesus's teachings that evening, Nicodemus replied, "How can this be?" (3:9). This does not necessarily imply he was cynical. Rather, it means he needed time to process before committing.

Readers experience Nicodemus again in John 7. Time has passed, and the chief priests and Pharisees are debating as to why Jesus has yet to be arrested. Nicodemus takes a risk to vocalize his thoughts: "Our law does not judge people without first giving them a hearing to find out what they are doing, does it?" (7:51 NRSV). The reader observes someone who was previously a withdrawn, inquisitive seeker becoming someone who is willing to thoughtfully counter the powers in the room. When Fives hold core convictions, they can be among the most compelling and powerful people in the world because of their capacity to support their case through careful reasoning and argumentation. Not surprisingly, Fives often make great lawyers, professors, and writers.

The last place in John's Gospel where the reader encounters the narrative of Nicodemus is chapter 19. Jesus has been crucified, and Nicodemus joins Joseph of Arimathea to take care of his body (19:38–40). "We can infer," say Tolomeo, Gervais, and De Roo, "that Nicodemus had not agreed to the council's decision to arrest and kill Jesus . . . [and that] he could no longer observe . . . but would now be one who was himself watched."[19] The man who first came to Jesus in the dark is willing to walk in the light of his new convictions that Jesus is the Messiah. This is nothing less than a startling transformation that is evidenced by his actions. When Fives act, it means they are resolved and convicted. For Nicodemus, this is no mere gesture of kindness but a pledge of faith—a pledge of true commitment, given that the Messiah is now dead.

For Fives who seek to better understand their story alongside the biblical narrative, John 3, 7, and 19 provide incisive insight. The Scripture that Fives should commit to memory is Hebrews 11:32–40, a passage that encourages them to grapple with what it may physically cost to cognitively hold Christian convictions in a secular world. Truly, the way of Jesus eventually requires disciples to engage their bodies and hearts in service of what their minds hold to be true.

Type Six

One word: Questioner

Core narrative: Peter walking on water (Matthew 14:22–33)

Memory passage: 1 Peter 5:7

The big picture for Sixes is this: you can conquer your fear if you are willing to face it. The lion from *The Wizard of Oz* most assuredly was a Six on a quest for courage. From the Bible, Peter best exemplifies the life of a Six. Sixes can make great leaders. Although their chief vice is fear, healthy Sixes transform fear into courage and often accomplish great things with those around them. Sixes reside in the thinking triad.

Due to fear and insecurity, Sixes often distrust their own thoughts and thus seek rules and structures for guidance.[20] This can make Sixes principled, but it can also lead to the unintended consequence of Sixes distrusting their own decision-making. "Their vivid imaginations can often cause them to get caught up in potential harm or threat in a situation."[21]

No matter how one reads Jesus's famous passage about the keys to the kingdom of heaven, it is generally agreed that Peter, as the eldest, was the leader of the disciples and held that role to one degree or another throughout the remainder of his life. There are many examples in Peter's life that help identify his Enneagram type as a Six. When faced with a difficult decision, Sixes often will distract themselves with a less complicated matter to avoid the issue. Assessing Peter as a Six aids the reader in understanding why he would return to fishing after the crucifixion and before the resurrection. Fishing was a familiar task that offered Peter security within the initial quagmire of confusion, betrayal, and loss after Jesus's death. In Jesus, Peter "had finally found an authority he could trust . . . and with whom he felt safe and secure."[22] Even before the crucifixion, in spite of Peter's trust in Jesus, his fear was crippling. Once Jesus is taken into custody, Peter's security falls apart. Thinking he might himself be harmed, he flees the scene and allows his fears to take over, which leads to his three denials. The rooster crowing after the third denial serves as Peter's wake-up call.

In fear, Sixes seek to avoid. The irony of the Six is that they seek authority while distrusting authority. After the crucifixion, Peter is dumbstruck because the trust he placed in Jesus ostensibly failed him. Tolomeo, Gervais, and De Roo provide keen insight into this dynamic:

> The work of transformation for the Sixes consists of taking back the unquestioning allegiance they have given to an outside authority and putting it back into themselves. Jesus' encounter with Peter after the resurrection does this for Peter. By questioning Peter about his love, Jesus helps Peter to look within himself and

discover the love within him that is not offered solely in reaction to what is expected of him. Sixes who turn to their inner strength learn to act out of compliance to what they know from within rather than what they have been told by an external authority. After the encounter with Jesus, Peter is able to continue his discipleship out of his newly-found courage and love, even to the point of ultimately suffering martyrdom.[23]

To be clear, this is not suggesting that Sixes look within for the ultimate source of truth in the way a New Age philosophy might prescribe. Rather, the Christian journey toward courage is to cultivate hearing God's voice within and to act boldly out of what one hears. This is why the deep work of prayer is imperative for the Six. The gift of Peter's narrative from the Bible is that readers encounter a young, recklessly naive follower of Jesus who matures over decades into a healthy, transformed man of courage.

One of the most famous accounts of Peter's life is when he comes to Jesus on the water. Recorded in Matthew 14, this scene depicts Peter as the counterphobic Six who naively jettisons the safety of the boat and walks on water toward Jesus. What is incredible about the account is that walking on water is Peter's own idea. None of the other disciples think of going out to Jesus, not even "the disciple whom Jesus loved." However, in getting out of the boat, Peter first seeks authority to do so.

> "Lord, if it's you," Peter replied, "tell me to come to you on the water."
> "Come," [Jesus] said. (Matt. 14:28–29)

Yet, as often happens with Sixes, when the waves grow in size, Peter's fear likewise grows, causing him to shrink back from his original inspiration. External circumstances can be paralyzing for Sixes. What began with fixating on Christ devolves into focusing on externals, and Peter sinks. In the moment of sinking,

Peter cries out to be saved. And, the text says, "immediately Jesus reached out his hand and caught him" (14:31). Against self-reliance and pop spirituality, the takeaway for the Christian is not to trust oneself but to trust the activity of God's presence within.

Peter is saved not by recovering positive thoughts or envisioning optimistic outcomes but by crying out for Jesus to save him, for God to act. The Christian's dependence is still on Christ, but in such a way that one must participate and act with God rather than passively wait. If Peter had not cried out, perhaps he would have continued to sink to the bottom of the sea in self-reliance. When one looks at the span of Peter's life in the Scriptures, what is evident is that the Peter who learned to trust in God who had come in flesh later had to trust in God, who sent the Spirit. The task for the Six today is to cultivate awareness of the voice of God, who leads and guides in the midst of chaotic circumstances. One psalmist reminds readers that God makes known the paths of life (Ps. 16:11). In due time God reveals all knowledge in order to walk in the way of mystery. Sadly, many Sixes never mature to this point. Yet those who do mature learn the lifelong task of casting their anxieties and fears on God because God cares (1 Pet. 5:7).

Type Seven

One word: Enthusiast

Core narrative: Solomon

Memory passage: Ecclesiastes 3:1

The big picture for Sevens is this: life is short, so face your pain. Also known as the enthusiast, the Seven is located in the thinking triad (see the appendix for more on the triads). As stated in chapter 2, Sevens are outwardly happy, but often inwardly sad due to painful experiences. The biblical character that Sevens may most identify with is King Solomon from the Hebrew Bible. Sevens often use busyness as a way to avoid "any direct confrontation with their inner wounds," according to Tolomeo, Gervais, and De Roo.[24] They also seek some level of mastery over the pleasures they ardently pursue.

Recalling that Sevens reside in the thinking triad helps shed light on Solomon's motives and behavior. When David passed the baton to Solomon to reign over Israel (1 Kings 2–3), Solomon wasn't sure what exactly to do next. Acting out of his thinking center, he decided to go to Mt. Gibeon, where he would offer extravagant sacrifices to God. Ultimately, God did not require Solomon to perform this sacrificial act, but in Solomon's intentions we catch an early glimpse of his excessive nature, something that became clearer in his life as time went on.

The breakthrough for Solomon came not while he was offering sacrifices he thought would be pleasing to God, nor even while Solomon was awake. Instead, it came in the dead of his sleep. During sleep, our mental and physical centers shut down, while the feeling center remains engaged. It is this center that permits one to dream. While Solomon sleeps, God asks him what he wants. His response is to ask for wisdom to rule the people (1 Kings 3:5–9). Tolomeo, Gervais, and De Roo note, "With his preferred ways of knowing closed off, Solomon is able to quickly access his feelings. His reply to God comes not from the head but from the heart."[25] The significance of this insight is that Sevens, who often suppress feelings, frequently make life decisions without being in touch with their deepest desires. This is why many Sevens wrestle with addiction, anxiety, and excessive outward behavior. Wisdom was unlocked when Solomon got out of his thinking center and into the feeling center. Healthy Sevens are able to face their pain and seek healing in order to apply what they feel to what they think in any given situation.

In one specific example, Solomon's wisdom is put to the test when two women seek his resolution of their dispute over which of them is the actual biological mother of a child (1 Kings 3:16–28). Ordering that the child be cut in half and each woman receive a portion proved to be the decisive action that revealed the true mother. Solomon settled the matter not through debate or cognitive reasoning but through an emotional appeal. This is a characteristic of a healthy Seven, who understands that feelings carry value and should not be neglected, numbed out, or glossed over through excessive behavior.

Solomon demonstrated Seven characteristics in his preoccupation with planning toward the future. His vision for the temple was beyond comprehension to his listeners (1 Kings 9:10–26). Even the Queen of Sheba was impressed. Surrounding nations all took notice of Israel's power, wealth, and religious supremacy (10:23–24). He imported twelve thousand horses from Egypt, built fleets of ships as never before, imported gold, maintained fourteen thousand chariots, and loved upwards of a thousand women—many of them from foreign nations.

Indulgence, as is often the case for Sevens, was Solomon's downfall. Toward the end of Ecclesiastes, he mourns that all these pursuits pale in meaning when compared to the eternal God. Some speculate that Solomon's many wives served as a defense against inner emptiness.[26] Whatever form a Seven's excessive pursuits take, the result is always the same: meaninglessness. What is vital for the Seven is a willingness to face pain. For a Seven who avoids pain at all costs, in the end the cost will only increase in weight, resulting in humiliation, despair, and for some, suicidal tendencies.

The Scripture memory verse for a Seven is Ecclesiastes 3:1, in which the author reminds the reader that everything in life has an appropriate time. The implication of this is that not every time is appropriate for everything. All things in moderation deserve a rightful place in a proper context. Ecclesiastes attests that Solomon grew in maturity from experience. As Tolomeo, Gervais, and De Roo put it, "He learned that weeping is as necessary as laughing and that his feelings can support and not undermine his work."[27] The reader learns that Solomon rejects avoidance as a survival strategy. Solomon learns that a life of distraction and excessive behavior is not the path to flourishing. Sevens would do well to heed Solomon's narrative in 1 Kings and to study Ecclesiastes as a glimpse of where an intemperate life leads.

Type Eight

One word: Challenger

Core narrative: Syrophoenician (Canaanite) woman (Matthew 15:21–28; Mark 7:24–30)

Memory passage: Proverbs 3:5–6

The big picture for Eights is this: your passion for justice is good, but self-reliance and sheer activism will only lead to soul fatigue, bitterness, and a weary heart. Eights are strong people. Decisive, bold, and justice-centered, Eights are located in the body or feeling triad (see the appendix for more on this). Their power can often be mistaken for self-assertion when, in reality, its object is not themselves but someone else. Eights do not necessarily seek to be in control, but they do seek to avoid being under the control of another. In the New Testament, both Martha and the Syrophoenician woman exhibit an Eight energy. Neither is afraid to confront Jesus; both confront him on behalf of justice done toward another, and both appear bold and self-confident. These traits from women, particularly women in antiquity, strike readers as exceptional and awkward because they undermine traditional notions of femininity. Further, Tolomeo, Gervais, and De Roo encourage us to reconsider our tendency to see the behavior of Eights as ungodly: "People who can only imagine a gentle, unchallenging God might want to dismiss the confrontational power of Eights as lesser channels of the Divine. The Eights, however, bring to our attention the strong, powerful and just side of the divine presence in our world. In so doing, they become clear manifestations of Holy Truth."[28] Eights are easily the most misunderstood type.

This work will focus the core Eight narrative on the Syrophoenician woman (Mark 7:24–30). The Gospel account of the encounter between Jesus and the Syrophoenician woman is awkward at best. Jesus seeks to remain away from the crowds when he arrives in the region of Tyre. Yet the woman, whose daughter had an unclean spirit, hears that he has arrived and bursts onto the scene to bow at his feet. This was probably not the quiet evening for which Jesus was hoping. As she begs for the release of the demon's stronghold, Jesus awkwardly refuses, stating that the children, presumably the descendants of Israel, must be fed before the dogs, implying the Gentiles. To the average contemporary reader, this image of Jesus doesn't align with traditional conceptions of the Jesus who came to heal, forgive, and restore all who asked of him.

Yet the woman refuses to let injustice win. She fights for her cause and challenges the Son of God that even dogs eat the scraps from the children's table. By pushing for justice, she is noting that there is enough power for even the Gentiles to get in on Jesus's restorative work. Spellbound by her faith, Jesus pronounces the daughter, who is not present, healed that very moment. And it was so.

The narrative highlights the Syrophoenician woman's directness, readiness for debate, and passion for justice.[29] She is depicted as strong, resolved, and willing to confront even a man whose social and spiritual power were clearly greater than her own. She does not appear to want control in the form of receiving the power to heal the daughter herself. Instead, she wants to channel the power of Jesus toward the expulsion of demonic activity in her daughter. Eights are typically willing to pay the price for what they deem valuable. In this case, she risks her reputation and social nicety to demand justice for her daughter. The woman refuses to take no as an answer. Pragmatically wired, she does not attempt to correct Jesus's ethnic discrimination (if that is, in fact, what occurred); instead, she employs a strategy to fit within his construct in order to get what she wants—a brilliant strategy that demonstrates an Eight's mentality.

One of the gifts of the Eight is a big heart. Although misunderstood at times, Eights seek truth above all. One of the distinct differences between an unhealthy and a healthy Eight is the basic desire to remain self-reliant.[30] The Syrophoenician woman, in desperation, became healthy when reaching out to Jesus for help. This is not an easy thing for Eights to do. Eights should remember that transformation is often most available when at a dead end, for it requires the assistance of others.

The final aspect to note is the theme of fairness. Fairness is a primary value for the Eight. Both Jesus and the woman argue for what they think is fair. After the woman pleads her case of fairness concerning the exorcisms, Jesus is willing to concede and grant her the request. Eights are most assertive and dominant when engaging issues pertaining to fairness, justice, and truth seeking. This is the case with the Syrophoenician woman. As Tolomeo, Gervais, and De Roo write, "The woman shows the Eight's forthrightness in not being concerned with public opinion when there are urgent things to be done. . . . Her heart motivates her to become protector of the weak."[31] The core takeaway from this passage for Eights is to trust God and not the self. God in due time feeds the hungry, clothes the sick, and provides rest for the brokenhearted. At the same time, God works through humans to mediate this love and compassion. Eights must learn to take action, but not outside of God's leading.

> ### Type Nine
>
> **One word:** Peacemaker
>
> **Core narrative:** Abraham (Genesis 12–25)
>
> **Memory passage:** Joshua 1:7–8

The big picture for the Nine is this: commit to the journey of self-discovery and act on your convictions. Nines are the mediators and peacemakers in this world. They reside in the intuitive triad and seem to possess a universal benevolence. They are "comforting, unselfish, and accommodating."[32] Due to their ardent desire for peace, they may avoid conflict at all costs and seek stability in circumstances and relationships. Unhealthy Nines are perceived as slothful and passive, hoping undesirable circumstances will take care of themselves. This is often due to a lack of clear vision, conviction, and direction. At their worst, Nines are lazy in their pursuit of transformation. The memory verse that Nines should commit to is Joshua 1:7–8: "Be strong and very courageous. Be careful to obey all the law my servant Moses gave you; do not turn from it to the right or to the left, that you may be successful wherever you go. Keep this Book of the Law always on your lips; meditate on it day and night, so that you may be careful to do everything written in it. Then you will be prosperous and successful." Boldness and conviction are imperative for Nines as they embark on the journey of transformation.

Although the journey Abraham is called by God to set out on is of national import, it is first a journey of personal discovery. There are six key moments (or scenes) in Abraham's pilgrimage that express classic Nine characteristics. The first scene of his journey is significant. Beginning in Genesis 12, after living seventy-five years in the same location (not unusual for a Nine), Abraham leaves, taking his family on an uncertain journey. His inner monologue is obviously not included in the biblical text, but the text states simply that Abraham obeyed and left his life of familiarity. We see the significance of this in Genesis 12:1, where God commands him to "go," which in Hebrew can also be translated as "go to yourself."[33] Although not the common interpretation, it is a plausible reading. This first scene demonstrates Abraham's willingness to embark on a journey of transformation. With slothfulness as their primary vice, an unhealthy Nine would have resisted the call and remained in the land of familiarity.

The second scene in Abraham's narrative occurs when he and Sarah arrive in Egypt to escape famine (Gen. 12). They fear that Pharaoh will kill Abraham if he discovers that Sarah, who is beautiful, is his wife. Determined to mislead Pharaoh into believing that Sarah is his sister, Abraham seeks to avoid conflict at all costs, to the point of compromising the truth. Eventually the truth comes out, and Pharaoh sends them away with their lives. The third scene occurs in Genesis 13, where Lot and Abraham part ways because of their increasing fruitfulness within geographical constraints. Abraham says to Lot, "Let there be no strife between you and me, and between your herders and my herders" (13:8 NRSV). He desires to maintain peace to the extent of permitting Lot to choose whatever direction he desires. Abraham, then, will go the other way.

Nines will usually preserve the peace, even if it means settling for a lesser-than reality. Moreover, they are often out of touch with what they themselves want. In Genesis 15, the fourth scene occurs. Abraham and Sarah are still barren, having yet to receive God's promise to establish a lineage. Sarah hatches a plan to have Hagar, the housemaiden, birth a child for Abraham in order to continue his line. Soon after, she becomes jealous of Hagar and instructs Abraham to cast her out. As in times past, Abraham listens to her and goes along with the plan according to her desires. Once again, Abraham avoids doing the right thing in order to keep the peace.

By Genesis 17, nearly a quarter century has passed, and Abraham has no lineage with Sarah as matriarch. Nines characteristically show patience, and this trait in Abraham is a stark juxtaposition to Sarah's personality. The fifth scene displaying a Nine identification comes from Genesis 18. Learning that God plans to annihilate Sodom for its godlessness, Abraham pleads on behalf of Lot's territory for its preservation. Like many Nines, he assumes a mediation role, attempting to forge peace between God and the many civilians who will imminently lose their lives.

The sixth and final scene that links Abraham with type Nine is in Genesis 22, one of the most bizarre and mysterious chapters in all of Scripture. Abraham is instructed to sacrifice Isaac, his own son and the only child of Sarah. In Jewish oral tradition, some posit that Abraham was a maker of idols in his younger days. Thus, this was the final test of whether he trusted the living God or sought to fashion God according to his own desires. Passing the test, Abraham moves to sacrifice Isaac, and just before he plunges the knife, God steps in and supplies a ram. Just as Abraham's journey as a Nine began with self-discovery, so it ends with his full transformation.

Without a doubt, Abraham learns to trust the voice of God and to act when called upon. By the end of his life, Abraham is fully aware of who he is: "Abraham and Sarah's journey is our own, giving up the familiar lands we know and moving to a place of trusting and connecting with our true selves and with God."[34]

If Jesus is Lord . . . any gospel which does not embrace both evangelism and social action is a counterfeit.

—N. T. Wright

Go home to your own people and tell them how much the Lord has done for you, and how he has had mercy on you.

—Mark 5:19

> **SKEPTIC'S QUESTION: Isn't the Enneagram a New Age tool?**
>
> **RESPONSE: No, it's a human tool that Christians can use to deepen faith and invite others into God's story of healing the world's brokenness.**

"Did anyone go witnessing this week?" the pastor asked with an ever-so-slight hint of religious condescension. All two hundred of us stared down into the gray carpet. I furtively glanced up to take a hand count. Zero.

I was twenty years old, working at a local church, passionate for Jesus, and committed to life in God's kingdom. It was the launch of a new young adult ministry led by my then boss. He went on to preach at us that if we truly loved Jesus we would be more willing to share our faith on the college campus. Easy for him to say, burrowed deep in the comforts of his office five days a week.

To emerging generations, evangelism is a dirty word. But it shouldn't be. Listening to that pastor, I started to wonder whether evangelism was a lost art. Or maybe it was like an ancient relic that had lost its luster and long since been forgotten.

The Enneagram can help us rediscover evangelism and its biblical roots. It can give us a common language to be able to meet people where they are, to open the hearts of those around us who are in search of life's deeper meaning.

What both evangelism and the Enneagram share in common is the presupposition that life is beautiful but also broken—systemically, corporately, and globally, but also individually, personally, and locally. The latter ripples out to affect the former. We will not see the systems of the world healed until personal healing and transformation take place, for the simple reason that systems are made of individual humans coming together. So maybe Christians should once again care about the craft of evangelism, particularly if we hold that Jesus is the answer to the world's brokenness. But we should probably start by rethinking the way we engage others, in order to avoid reducing people to projects.

Holdings

An overlooked aspect of the Enneagram is a concept called "holdings." In all my gleanings from Enneagram experts, few ever talk about this concept. It has been one of my most significant discoveries. Remember, the Enneagram is a tool that "maps the various ways the ego develops to deal with the absence, disruptions, ruptures, and discontinuities of holding."[1] Holdings are the various ways we subconsciously attempt to put the world back together. It looks differently for each type, but the inner conviction is the same:

The world is broken. It needs mending. How can I help?

According to Enneagram expert Sandra Maitri, "The nine Ennea-types arise out of reaction to the loss of our basic trust and concomitant disconnection from being."[2] Portions of our personalities, then, are formed because of woundings, or what the Christian tradition might call the fall. Because of sin's entrance into the world, the human race seeks to "hold" situations in various ways as a strategy to restabilize our reality. Holdings are ways we cope, manage, and attempt to succeed in life, within all of life's brokenness.

Kuwaiti American author A. H. Almaas attaches specific holdings to each Enneatype. Each holding describes a subconscious strategy employed to fix the world.

Type One: In a broken world, I will triumph through self-improvement.

Type Two: In a broken world, I will serve in order to get others to accept me.

Type Three: In a broken world, I will develop myself to make success happen.

Type Four: In a broken world, I will feel its pangs and mourn with it.

Type Five: In a broken world, I will isolate myself to solve problems.

Type Six: In a broken world, I will become fearfully paranoid about the potential dangers.

Type Seven: In a broken world, I will avoid its pain through denial and seeking pleasure.

Type Eight: In a broken world, I will fight for justice through anger at the fall.

Type Nine: In a broken world, I will make it better through routine and calm.[3]

Like the Greek god Atlas, consigned to balance the weight of heaven on his shoulders, holdings suggest that we are each attempting, consciously or subconsciously, to balance the world's weight on our own shoulders. We try to fix the world's brokenness in unique ways through our personalities. This isn't necessarily a bad thing. It simply underscores that we are aware of the world's brokenness, that we seek to mend the gap, and that our personalities play a role in how we attempt to accomplish that. Brokenness, then, is a place where we can find common ground in the public square.

Judaism offers a wonderful perspective on our role in healing social and societal brokenness: *tikkun olam*, which means "to repair the world." We are brought into the family of God not merely as recipients but also as participants, each of us with a unique role in joining God in the great renewal. This means that, despite our differences in worldview, philosophy, religion, and faith, the vast majority of people can agree that the world is not as it should be, that our workplaces and neighborhoods are in need of renewal, that there is still good work to be done in reconciliation and relationship building with our families and friends, and that our inner lives are not as whole as we desire them to be.

To admit the truth that we are broken is a gift—and a release of the burden that phony self-righteousness brings upon us. We do not need to pretend. To deny our common brokenness is to live in illusion. Have you watched the evening news recently? Or followed the thread of a recent Twitter spat? Or taken note of your own inner monologue when you were last cut off in traffic?

We are not whole.

And here is the silver lining to that grim reality: we can all agree on brokenness. It is in our common brokenness that evangelism can and should begin. Evangelism must begin not where we disagree on matters of doctrine but where we agree on common longings. And it is painfully obvious that the world is not the way it was intended to be; we ourselves are not as we were intended to be. Let's start there.

We can all agree that our political discourse is broken. We can all agree that many of our institutions are broken, that discrimination, inequality, and privilege are alive and well. We can all agree that anxiety, fear, and depression are anything but in decline. Our common confession, then, is that we are individually broken. The Enneagram affirms this confession. We are beautiful, and we are broken.

Cheap Language

Something can be bankrupt yet still carry value. For something to be bankrupt means that it lacks the value it once held. Language works this way. Language can become bankrupt. It's often difficult for me, an American living in the twenty-first century, to comprehend the depths of Shakespeare's verse. Slang also works this way. No one with cultural credibility still says "groovy" when referring to something they like. You'd simply think to yourself that they are either culturally irrelevant or have been frozen in time since 1973.

Jonathan Merritt illustrates this clearly in *Learning to Speak God from Scratch*, in which he explores the challenge of speaking about God in a world where language is rapidly changing. In a previous age we could walk up to the water cooler at work and talk about sin. We could host a neighborhood party and work biblical concepts like "sin," "salvation," and "grace" into everyday dialogue. But, at least in the modern West, that ship has sailed. For our evangelism efforts to be effective, we must begin where we agree, using words that carry currency across diverse worldviews. Words such as "sin" and "fall" import all sorts of traumatic baggage that conjure shaming, condescension, and cliché in hearers. These are usually not the places to begin.

Beauty is a place to begin. Brokenness is a place to begin. The Enneagram itself is a place to begin as people are typically open to self-discovery, to seeing their own beauty but also their own brokenness. This is why the Enneagram must never be an end in itself. It is always a means to unlock more of this grand mystery we call life.

"Tell all the truth but tell it slant." Emily Dickinson opened a universe of wisdom with this line of poetry. Jesus often told the truth slant. This is why the parables were so effective. Through the parables Jesus was able to reaffirm ancient truth, but through the back door. I have found that the Enneagram is a slanted and thus effective approach to evangelism. It helps us gain credibility and commonality with people from diverse backgrounds. It helps us get to ultimate truth, but in a slanted direction.

To summarize what this chapter has stressed thus far:

1. The Enneagram is a tool that, increasingly, is becoming common language in the public square.
2. The Enneagram helps us name both the beauty *and* the brokenness of ourselves and the world, which we are consciously or subconsciously working to mend.
3. The Enneagram is a slanted way to help us get at the core truth of our need for redemption from a source beyond ourselves.

It is essential at this stage for us as followers of Jesus to begin with our own brokenness. We do not come at evangelism as perfected saints who have sorted out all divine mysteries. Rather, we speak of the ways we have been healed, are being healed, and are pursuing healing in the world through life *in Christ*. I've observed that when I start with the Enneagram instead of with concepts such as sin and death, across the table I notice eyes opening, ears perking up, and a dialogue beginning. It is here in our brokenness—where we agree—that I often most sense God's beginning movement in the life of another.

For many readers, particularly those who live in an urban context, this will seem like common sense. But there are many followers of Jesus who believe the Enneagram leads adherents to the realm of Satan. I'd like to briefly address that (erroneous) assumption. First, let's dispel the notion that the Enneagram is a Christian theory. It is not. The Enneagram is not Jesus, nor will it ever be. One need not know the Enneagram to experience the divine life that Christ offers us. But neither is it a New Age theory. Rather, it is a human theory. Just as God once used the stars in the sky to guide Eastern spiritualists—the Magi—to find and worship Jesus, so God can use human personality theories like the Enneagram to help make the gospel accessible in a skeptical world. The simple truth is that God meets people where they are, rather than where we may want them to be. And the Enneagram can be a tool to meet people where they are.

I've seen this happen firsthand. I know many who have given up on faith, the church, the Messiah, and so forth, but are willing to attend an Enneagram workshop. And within that context the Holy Spirit can begin anew, eventually leading that person back to a recognition that there is no salvation found within the gods of self-help, consumerism, and self-actualization.

Second, the origins of the Enneagram are unknown. But when one studies the desert fathers, and in particular Evagrius of Pontus, overlap with the core Enneagram theory becomes obvious. And here is the fascinating part: Evagrius is the theologian to whom we attribute the notion of the seven deadly sins. Isn't that interesting? Evagrius wanted to help his disciples grasp the nature of their brokenness (i.e., sin), but he wanted to tell this truth slant.

Here is an example to illustrate why this is important: On occasion, a church will cancel a workshop that it scheduled me to lead. Inevitably, it is canceled not because no one registered but because a few people in the church fear that the Enneagram opens people up to New Age spirituality. It usually starts with a pastor whose desire is to help their congregation grow deeper, which is exactly the work I do—using the Enneagram as a tool to help Christians create a discipleship pathway based on their unique personality. But once the registration goes live, a vocal minority will submit emails, voicemails, and unsolicited feedback letting the pastor know that if he or she brings the Enneagram into the church, the pagan pentagram won't be far behind. It's silly, and thankfully it doesn't happen often, but I am saddened when it does.

This saddens me because often it is these kinds of churches that are most in need of fresh tools for evangelizing an ever-changing world. It is churches like these that often refuse to learn the language being used in the public square. Instead, they approach evangelism with bankrupt terminology while treating their subject as merely a project to convert. It's no wonder evangelism has become a dirty word.[4]

Our attempts to share the good news of God in Christ must arise from a posture of being *for* the other and not *against* the other. When people step into evangelism and hold an *against* posture, this is painfully obvious to the human sitting across the table—someone who, by the way, is an image bearer of God. Evangelism at its best dignifies the other person without needing to objectify them as a project. In evangelism one realizes that, no matter the outcome, the person in front of us is already a bearer of God's image. Healthy evangelism that fits within Jesus's commission recognizes that each person has a transformative story to tell—a faith worth bearing witness to—and refuses to shove truth down someone else's soul or to divorce their sharing of the gospel from authentic relational invitation. Author Frank Viola reminds us, "In the first century, the words 'gospel' and 'evangelize' referred to heralding the good news that a new emperor had been installed in the Roman Empire. Heralds would go out to proclaim the good news, informing people that a new era of peace, salvation, and blessing had begun. They then exhorted people to get down on their knees to worship the new emperor. The apostles used this same language to describe the preaching of the gospel of Jesus Christ."[5]

Christ is our King. *He* runs the world—not the president, not our nation, and certainly not our favorite sports team. We bear witness to Jesus's reign over our life and the life of the world. To humbly correct my former boss at that worship gathering long ago, we don't "go witnessing." Rather, we bear witness out of an encounter with the living God. We are heralds, not yellers—seeking to speak truthfully, not forcefully, and to bear witness, not win arguments. It is in the sharing of our transformative stories with another that the Holy Spirit grips human hearts. Evangelism happens when, like a water brook, God's presence wells up inside us and starts to overflow into our relationships and conversations. This is also how Christian faith has always been shared. The Enneagram can help because it has become common in the public square (transcending many faiths, worldviews, and cultures) and because it names our common brokenness that manifests through personality patterns.

Through the Enneagram I have been able to help others name where they are subconsciously attempting to balance the world through their "holding." Holdings are actually exhausting. We cannot do it. We are broken. But if we start with brokenness—where we agree—we can get honest about our anxiety, fear, frustration, and fatigue. This serves as a critical launching point from which we can then humbly offer a way forward that connects us to healing, power, and renewal in the person of Jesus. Jesus never intended for us to put the world back together on our own. Abiding is critical if we are to make the long journey of inner healing, outer justice, and mercy. Many people are just now beginning to awaken to the hard truth that the healing we desire can't be found in the places we've been looking: in individualism, in consumerism, in careerism, in self-help . . . not even in saging the house as a remedy for our chronic anxiety. None of it is working.

Truth is, the brokenness isn't just "out there"; it's also "in here." We are all a swirling cocktail, some parts beautiful and some parts broken, stirred all the way through. As singer-songwriter Derek Webb once wrote, "Good Lord, I'm crooked deep down."[6] Hip-hop artist Propaganda puts it this way: "It's crooked . . . Me, just a crooked stick in all of his goodness."[7]

If this offends you, or if you believe yourself to be the rare exception to the rule of human brokenness, consider this meditation: you've most likely consumed bugs, rodent hairs, and feces in your recent breakfast, lunch, and dinner. The US Food and Drug Administration legally permits up to nine rodent hairs for every sixteen-ounce box of spaghetti. The coffee beans you grind for breakfast are allowed to have an average of ten milligrams or more of animal poop per pound.[8] Lord, have mercy. The point is that even a milligram of brokenness is enough to make you rethink self-righteousness. To one degree or another, we are all broken. To every degree imaginable, we need healing.

The Enneagram helps us identify our specific areas of brokenness, recognize our holdings, and open our minds to the glaring possibility that we are not whole on our own. As Christians this is a starting point to humble evangelism. After all, Jesus's first words in his public ministry were not, "Hey, everybody. I'm not really sure I need to be here. Everything seems to be just fine here. Keep doing what you're doing." Instead, his first words were, "Repent, for the kingdom of heaven has come near" (Matt. 3:2). Or, to paraphrase: "Turn away from your broken pathways, for the reign of God's wholeness is upon you."

Our next step may then be to help someone wonder, as we once did, What story is big enough? What story is redemptive enough? What story is compelling and powerful enough to both eclipse the brokenness within me and renew the entire world? Jesus of Nazareth's story, of course.

Instead of asking, "Did anyone go witnessing this week?" maybe the better question to ask is, "Can I get a witness, anyone?"

practice

Create an intentional conversation with someone you know who is aware of the Enneagram and does not consider themselves a follower of Jesus. Consider the ways that talking about your type with them might provide an opening to share your personal brokenness and how life in Christ is specifically transforming you.

"Character" is the human equivalent of the writing that runs right through a stick of Brighton Rock.

—N. T. Wright

Whoever walks in integrity walks securely,
    but whoever takes crooked paths will be found out.

—Proverbs 10:9

> **SKEPTIC'S QUESTION:** Is it true that I am stuck with my number and should just make peace with the way I am?
>
> **RESPONSE:** You have all Enneatypes in you. Becoming healthy within your core type will require effort in the form of spiritual practices and engagement.

In one of the more striking metaphors I've heard, Anglican theologian and former bishop N. T. Wright compares Christian character to a certain British candy. Although "rock candy," as it's sometimes called, looks like a regular candy cane, it is no mere stick of sugar. On each end of the stick reads the phrase "Brighton Rock." If you were to cut the stick down the middle, the newly cut ends would still read "Brighton Rock." Simply put, words on each end have been wondrously (and somewhat mysteriously) diffused through the entire sugar stick. As Wright notes, what you see on the outside of the stick matches what you find on the inside.

character creating a rule of life for wholeness

We've all been around people who act one way within a certain environment and then live out completely different values within another. Maybe you do that. Maybe I do too. Some refer to this as being "two-faced" or hypocritical, which historically meant to wear a mask, putting on the appearance of virtue and never revealing one's true, fallen self. It is the opposite of integrity. It is the inverse of character. When a building has integrity or is noted for good character, its structure is consistent and stable from the foundation to the roof. The same applies to humans. To be a person of character is to bear integrity all the way through. Rather than wavering values and virtues from moment to moment, those with good character consistently present themselves in the same manner, regardless of context.

Rock candy is like this. No matter where you cut it, the words remain the same. Wright says, "I don't actually know how Brighton Rock . . . is manufactured, but an ordinary stick doesn't automatically have writing that goes all the way through."[1] The inventor of rock candy intentionally diffused the words through it. Character is the same. No one becomes like Jesus by accident. It is always a result of radical intention.

We come into the family of God through grace. But we are made Christlike through practice. As Dallas Willard so wonderfully puts it, "Grace is not opposed to effort, but to earning. Earning is an attitude. Effort is an action. Grace, you know, does not just have to do with forgiveness of sins alone."[2] Make no mistake: life will eventually "cut" you down the middle, like a stick of Brighton Rock. And what you see as a result of the cut is who you are. It's when we get below the surface and see a core that doesn't match the exterior that we know we still have work to do.[3]

The Enneagram is a helpful tool to reveal specific areas of brokenness that need effort as we seek to become people of integrity. Christians invite the Holy Spirit to transform them as they commit to spiritual practices over time to develop character. Much of the work we must do is undoing wounds of our past—both things we've done and things done to us. In recent years, neuroscience has helped us better understand the plasticity (or agility) of our brains. Our neurological connections move along paths of least resistance, which means that the more you think about or do something, the more default it will become over time. Like tire tracks pressing down a trail, our brain connections are formed through consistent pressing down over time. If we want to change our default patterns of thinking and behaving, we will need to exert effort to rewire connections, lest we tread down default paths of destruction.

Miracle on the Hudson?

On the afternoon of January 15, 2009, I received a text message telling me to turn on the news because something unusual was happening in Manhattan. As a result of 9/11, my instincts reflexively braced for tragedy. Instead, the report revealed a spectacular event involving an airplane landing on the Hudson River. The chyron on the bottom of the screen read, "Miracle on the Hudson." Soon after its takeoff from LaGuardia Airport, US Airways flight 1549 encountered a flock of Canada geese, some of which flew into the plane's engines and caused them to fail. Unsure whether the plane could safely return to the airport for an emergency landing, pilot Chesley "Sully" Sullenberger and copilot Jeffrey Skiles determined to glide the plane onto the Hudson River instead. No biggie, right?

The video feed—featuring a massive airbus resting on the water's surface, passengers standing on its wings—was bizarre, to say the least. For days it was the subject of conversations, even in Los Angeles, where I was living at the time. The word that most people used to describe the event was "miracle." I mean, who glides a commercial airplane carrying 155 passengers onto a river? From many people's perspective, it was a miracle. Weeks later, however, reflecting on the events of that day, Sullenberger shared that he did not view it this way.

For years, prior to his courageous act that saved his passengers, Sully had made a hobby out of the practice of gliding. In gliding, a pilot cooperates with the wind to steer a vessel toward a destination. Although Sully had never specifically practiced gliding a commercial airplane, when the moment of crisis arrived, his instincts took over.

Spiritual formation works like this.[4] The habits we form end up forming us. The idea of "rising to the occasion" is false. Few if any of us can actually rise to the occasion when times are hard; instead, most of us default to our highest level of previous training.

If you want to have more patience in the evening with your kids, learn to sit patiently in the morning with your God. If you want to experience joy within a season of darkness, create a daily habit of capturing gratitude in order to reshape your outlook. If you want to break a habit of viewing pornography, create new habits that orient you toward a better story and take strategic action to prevent access in times of temptation. It all sounds simple, yet it is in the simple, rhythmic habits that our minds are renewed, longings reoriented, and virtue restored. Sully's countless hours of gliding landed him safely on the Hudson. The practices we commit to can end up saving our marriages, our friendships, and even our own souls. It is vital to take these practices seriously, then, because it is in our commitment to the little things that the presence of God is able to conform us to the image of Christ.

Connecting Type with Character

Every Enneagram type centers in a core vice and a corresponding virtue.

	Vice	Virtue
Type 1	Anger	Serenity
Type 2	Pride	Humility
Type 3	Deceit	Truthfulness
Type 4	Envy	Emotional Balance
Type 5	Greed	Nonattachment
Type 6	Fear	Courage
Type 7	Gluttony	Sobriety
Type 8	Lust	Innocence
Type 9	Apathy	Action

This is not to say that the core vice per type is the only one, or that the core virtue is the only virtue one should seek. Rather, it is to help identify areas that are natural defaults and propensities and to name specifically the kinds of people we want to become in order to imitate Christ.

These are not comprehensive but provide the initial vision to begin the work of naming growth areas once you've discovered your Enneagram type. For example, Sixes more naturally wrestle with fear and therefore must aim to develop courage. This, then, should inform Sixes' spiritual practices. Nines are most tempted by apathy and must resist the urge to become passive. Therefore, they should engage spiritual practices that summon attention and action. Threes default to the vice of deceit and should thus seek out practices to grow in authenticity. One's Enneagram type has much to do with spiritual practices of engagement. This is how character is formed.

Allow me to offer a personal example. I present as an Enneagram Three. I am aware that my default patterns of thinking are that I am never good enough and that I am only as "good" as my last teaching or how I performed in the recent pick-up basketball game. I am also insecure about whether you like this book. I am comfortable in a meritocratic society where we perform to become people of value. Therefore, I must habitually push against this default pattern by engaging practices like contemplative prayer and solitude, or else I will naturally veer into productivity and public opinion about my performance as a way of achieving self-worth and identity.

We all have default patterns of thinking and acting. Upstream practices are important in reshaping these patterns, but our tendency will be to try to avoid them for the simple reason that they push against our instincts. For integrity to mature, one must commit to three specific principles: aim, practices, and habits.

Aim

Everything begins with articulating your aim. Everything ends with it as well. Without an aim, our efforts drift into either the desert of wandering or the dredges of duty. In the desert of wandering, we struggle with stops and starts because we don't have a fixed target and are constantly changing our minds. The dredges of duty are even worse. Duty is that place you find yourself in when you stop and think, "Why am I doing this?" and "Who I am called to be?" Sometimes we go through the motions for years before stopping to ask these questions.

Questions that start with the words "why" and "who" are essential to human flourishing. If you only commit to questions that begin with "what" without knowing your "who," you can easily end up with a religious spirit that is bitter and cold.

Start there: Who do you want to be?

Name your aim here:

Aim (who)

For the Christian, the answer to this question is perhaps obvious. Our aim is to be Christlike. Becoming like Jesus is the ultimate aim of existence. As Scripture declares, "In this world we are like Jesus" (1 John 4:17). Unfortunately, we are not always like Jesus in this world, so our aim must be clear and compelling. If it's not clear, then we will drift. If it's not compelling, we will veer when life presents challenges. I am constantly reminding myself that cultivating the character of Christ far outweighs lesser loves that entice my desires. Each of us, no matter who we are or what our ultimate longing is, would do well to attempt to articulate our aim: the "who" or "why" of our existence. We will need to return to this aim again and again as a reminder that the difficult road we've taken to grow is worth it.

I encourage people to name a couple of virtues to cultivate in order to move toward their aim. Specificity is vital. Ambiguity never changes anything. To support your ongoing growth toward the "who," you need to next specify the "what." For example, perhaps being a parent has revealed that your patience is lacking. Or maybe you're a student and have come to realize that perseverance is a virtue that is imperative if you are going to finish your studies. In West Michigan, where I live, we receive less sunlight in the winter than perhaps any other region in the United States. Since weather does in fact play into our emotional health, a commitment to the virtue of joy is essential. (A robust list of virtues can be found in the appendix.)

What must you cultivate this season to advance toward your aim? Note that this will be a lifelong journey, so there's no need to pick more than two or three virtues per season. Some will find it helpful to merely focus on one over a period of time. Consider how your Enneagram type contributes to your particular default patterns of vice and temptation. What virtues should you seek in your growth journey?

Virtue 1 (what)	Virtue 2 (what)

Practices

Now that you have named your "who" and "what," you can get more practical. Practices are the "how" of character formation. Some refer to practices as disciplines. Recall from chapter 3 the recommended upstream and downstream practices for your Enneatype. If those are helpful, use them. (For a more comprehensive list of spiritual practices, refer to the appendix.) As you think about specific practices, select ones that are going to specifically help you cultivate the virtues you're pursuing. For example, joy often increases the more we connect ourselves with nature. If joy is a virtue you want to grow in, perhaps commit to praying as you walk through a nearby trail. Likewise, patience can increase when we seek solitude away from noise; if impatience is a temptation, commit to regular times of solitude when you will remove yourself from the presence of others and technology.

Practices are ways that humans can initiate contact with God while also surrendering to God within the discipline, in order to be transformed by grace. A simple example of this is Bible reading. One must actively open the Bible yet must passively be transformed through permitting God to reveal, convict, and restore when exposed to biblical truth. Humans are active in pursuing specific practices yet are passive in receiving power for transformative purposes. Therefore, spiritual disciplines are not just willful piety of human effort but are also willing practices in which God makes contact with us.

Upstream and downstream practices were offered above as a way to help each Enneatype think through how they are wired and what practices can guide them toward health. Consider implementing those practices or borrowing practices from another type. No matter which practices you select, be clear why you think they will cultivate deeper virtue toward your aim, and discern how your personality comes into play and can be shaped toward wholeness.

What practices would you like to commit to in this season?

Practice 1 (how)	Practice 2 (how)

Habits

Last but certainly not least, it is vital to create rhythms through which these practices are enacted. Good intentions that never cross into commitments of time and space remain merely intentions. And intentions alone are not transformative. When practices become routine and over time become habits, growth begins to happen. This is the "where" and "when" of character formation.

One of my heroes is Adele Calhoun. Part spiritual ninja, part Enneagram aficionado, Adele has faithfully counseled and pastored hundreds of disciples and has authored several works on spiritual formation. During a recent phone call, Adele offered a remarkable insight with regard to the Enneagram and spiritual practices: "It feels irrelevant to know your number if you're not going to work it." The Enneagram is helpful when we view it as a means toward transformation rather than an end to confine yourself and others to a number. You have to work spiritual practices consistently over time in order to see change and manifest growth and health within your type. No one goes to the gym after a three-year hiatus and expects immediate results. Bodily health takes time and habit. Spiritual health works the same way. It is in our habits that we rewire our neural pathways toward maturity.

Now that you are clear about your aim, have established virtues that will move you toward that aim, and have designated spiritual practices to help in your cultivation of these virtues, the next and final step is to commit to habits—the specific times and places through which you can begin to routinize your practices. Some people have a preferred time of day, a favorite chair, a particular lighting scheme, or a beloved wilderness path. All of those details are important. They give you a sense of agency and familiarity that is grounding. Attempt to connect the details of each habit to a specific practice. For example, if you sense it is time for a habit of daily Bible reading, mark the details of that habit under the reading practice.

Record a few of those details below:

_____	_____
_____	_____
Habit 1 (when and where)	Habit 2 (when and where)

The Presence We Seek

Many Christians I meet today come from traditions they now seek to avoid. In some cases this is understandable, but it is also unfortunate. Traditions pass down convictions of times past. To be sure, what starts out as a core conviction in one generation can sometimes devolve into legalism in another. For example, in the early 1900s, alcohol abuse was out of control. When churches took a stance to free people from addiction at that time, abstaining from alcohol became a core conviction. The Wesley brothers preached holiness, and teetotaling was a central practice that assured freedom from the cultural struggle within what became the Methodist tradition. Yet today, several generations later, cultural norms have shifted and churches that continue to prohibit alcohol consumption can be viewed as unnecessarily legalistic, especially given that the Bible does not explicitly condemn the use of alcohol (and in a few passages even seems to celebrate it). Rules over time must be reevaluated to ensure that they bring life—and not legalism—to any system, and that they serve the ultimate aim. This is what is happening in Acts 10 when Peter is given new insight into the kosher laws in light of the new covenant.

The phrase "rule of life" isn't always well received in church contexts, but often people's hesitation stems from a lack of understanding of what it really is. So then, let's clarify: a rule of life, or *regula* in Latin, is a commitment to consistently live out a way of life that is rooted in an ultimate aim. Without an aim, or when we lose sight of our aim, our practices become meaningless. Practices are always meant to serve the aim.

Take note that it is healthy to change your rule of life from season to season. Experiencing dryness from time to time is normal. Contrast and change can be life giving. Just as the seasons of change in weather patterns bring a welcome contrast (when summer changes to autumn, for example), so does changing our practices. The point is not to persist in a habit out of sheer stubbornness; it is to engage in habits that will support your practices and lead to the aim you seek. A rule of life allows for flexibility and change within the overarching and unchanging scope of your aim.

Remember, it is God and his presence that we seek. In his presence we are changed, and spiritual practices are pathways we choose in order to center ourselves in God's presence. We don't meditate on the Scriptures in order to simply know what the text says. We meditate on the Scriptures as an invitation for the Holy Spirit to meet us in that cosmic story. Likewise, we walk into nature not merely to admire the beauty of creation—as good as that is; we walk into nature to be restored to the Creator, who holds it all by hand. Practices are the means by which we seek the presence of God, who is our ultimate aim. And like any relationship, contrast is helpful so as not to get stuck in a rut. So give yourself permission to change it up.

Since you have already filled in the lines above, put it all together below so you can see how everything connects. And may God's Spirit meet you in those spaces as you commit to seeking God's presence through specific transformative practices.

Rule of Life (*Regula*)

Aim (who)

| Virtue 1 (what) | Virtue 2 (what) |

| Practice 1 (how) | Practice 2 (how) |

| Habit 1 (when and where) | Habit 2 (when and where) |

The aim of *The Enneagram for Spiritual Formation* is to situate the Enneagram properly within the Christian life. There are many who place entirely too much emphasis on the tool, believing it to be essential knowledge for human flourishing. Some may even treat it as a kind of psychological replacement for faith, which can lead to narcissism or despair. Others on the opposite end of the spectrum reject it altogether, conflating it with New Age spirituality or dismissing it due to its popularity among evangelicals.

This book takes a different path—a third way, if you will. The statements below are a final attempt to conclude this work with succinct articulation.

The Enneagram isn't Jesus, but it can help you learn how to be more like him.

The Gnostics of antiquity believed that special knowledge (*gnosis*) was the key to human flourishing. This knowledge was available only to select chosen ones, while the rest of humanity was consigned to ignorance and possible damnation. In my years working with this tool, there have been times when I've sensed a regard for the Enneagram comparable to the Gnostics' regard for secret knowledge. The language of the Enneagram can function like a brand of coded speech within communities of privilege, where insiders and outsiders are unintentionally formed based on their knowledge.

Properly put in its place, the Enneagram is a tool for self-awareness that helps to name tendencies where growth is necessary for spiritual maturity. The Enneagram is not an alternative religion, faith, or pathway. It is merely a tool. When engaging this tool, one becomes more aware of various patterns and able to choose specific practices that can transform one's mind, emotions, and body. The Enneagram can help lead us to Jesus, but it is never a replacement for vibrant faith in Christ.

The Enneagram won't save your marriage, but it can provide valuable insight into your relational dynamic.
Over the years, my wife, Elaina, and I have studied each other's type in order to better understand our marriage dynamic. This work has become a tremendous asset in navigating our differences. Rather than viewing one another's particularities with suspicion or confusion, we have grown to appreciate (and even laugh with) one another because of our unique proclivities. Along the way, the resources of the Enneagram Institute (www.enneagraminstitute.com) have helped us grow in our relationship.

I have learned that her Six wing causes her to fear the unknown. Ensuring that our house doors are locked at night and the security system has been set reflects not merely a preference but a strong need for security and safety. I now believe this predisposition has always been part of her personality and was most likely solidified at an early age. The Enneagram has helped me as a husband learn to honor her desire. (This has been a process, since I grew up in a household where we frequently left doors unlocked, day and night.)

Elaina has learned that, as a Three, I thrive on performance and feedback. Her opinions mean a great deal to me. Even though she is not one to overstate or share her opinion unsolicited, she has learned that I sincerely want to hear her thoughts and to connect with her opinions about my writing, teaching, and leadership. Over the years, she has committed to giving me regular feedback without me asking.

In sum, I am grateful for how the Enneagram has helped us self-reflect and navigate our longings so that we can better serve our relationship. I would not recommend the Enneagram in lieu of marriage counseling, but I would affirm it as an incredibly helpful tool to help any relationship grow.

The Enneagram isn't a guide to parenting, but it can help you understand the uniqueness of a child.

It's been stated that around age four, children begin to show patterns of behavior consistent with Enneagram types. Remember that the Enneagram journey of type discovery is one we each make for ourselves. Nevertheless, knowledge of each type can help parents understand why children are motivated differently and how to best lead them in the way they should go.

Elaina and I detected that our daughter, at about age five, presented perfectionist tendencies that were rooted in her desire to please us. This manifested with her being unreasonably critical of herself if she didn't excel quickly when engaging new activities. Rather than pushing her to try harder, the Enneagram has helped us understand some of her tendencies and gently invite her to consider that it is okay to *not* be perfect at something, particularly when one is first learning.

When I was a child, I was motivated by the exact opposite impulse as a presenting Three. I would receive the feedback to try harder as a wonderful invitation to achieve for my own well-being. But Elaina and I have learned that our daughter hears that invitation frustratingly and is self-critical because she seeks to please us, her parents. This changes everything in the way we encourage her in new activities.

Children are incredibly impressionable and vulnerable. The Enneagram has helped Elaina and me to step back, observe our daughter's behavior, discern her possible motives, and nurture her emotions as she matures. She is now six, and we have never discussed the Enneagram with her, nor have we attempted to type her. However, we do discern a few patterns of behavior she presents and are curious about several types that she manifests thus far. The Enneagram has been insightful to our journey of parenting.

The Enneagram won't increase your profit margin, but it can help you learn how to more effectively lead an organization.[1] Several times each year, the executive pastoral team at Mars Hill Bible Church gets away to talk through leadership and vision. Recently, we began to use the Enneagram as a way to explore our personal assets and liabilities in leadership. Too often our leadership biases remain undiagnosed and subconscious. The tragic reality of this is that these biases may remain unknown to us, but other people experience them and are often more aware of our own patterns of leadership than we are. Over time, these tendencies can negatively affect an organization's culture.

On a recent retreat, on the lakeshore of West Michigan (which I highly recommend between June and September), each of our executive leaders was asked to reflect on how our Enneatypes present when we lead from a place of health and how our Enneatypes present when we are unhealthy. The experience was both vulnerable and insightful, as we learned how we each function differently and ways we could create better meetings, have more transparent conversations, and encourage better self-care.

I have learned that Enneagram Fives show up to meetings very differently from Threes. The way Enneagram Eights engage conflict and resolution is quite different from Nines and Twos. When leaders understand the dynamics of diversity within their team, it can lead to heightened effectiveness, greater efficiency, and better organizational culture.

The Enneagram isn't salvific, but it can open spiritual conversations with those who do not yet know Jesus.

I am a big fan of Alpha, an evangelism tool developed by a church in London called Holy Trinity Brompton. One of the main reasons Alpha works is that it seeks to identify with skeptics as its first priority. When we meet people where they are and connect with who they are, bonds are formed because people feel seen, heard, and loved. This can naturally (and sometimes supernaturally) open hearts for further exploration because people feel existentially safe and secure.

I think the Enneagram is like that. In the chapter on evangelism, I sought to explain how the Enneagram is a neutralizer in conversation. I cannot overstate enough that the Enneagram is not a New Age tool, a Christian tool, or any brand of tool. It is a human tool. Therefore, it can create a shared conversation with anyone. It transcends race, religion, gender, class, sexuality, politics, and any other container we use to group people. I know a Seven who is white, agnostic, female, progressive, and middle class, and identifies as LGBTQ. I also know a Seven who is black, Christian, male, moderate, and upper class, and has been married to a woman for thirty years.

The Enneagram is a great neutralizer. It opens people up to relational exploration, self-discovery, and friendship. When we begin to form the bonds, a bridge is built between two people that can support the truth of the gospel—namely, that in life, death, and resurrection, the Son of God is renewing all things and reconciling hearts back to their Creator. It also opens new pathways for others to share what they deem most valuable to us. This is healthy for any friendship. It certainly beats being shouted down with Bible verses through a bullhorn. Whereas the Enneagram itself falls far short of the gospel, it is an entry point to begin fresh conversations and become curious together. This is a beautiful thing that the Holy Spirit can use to lead us toward incredible renewal over the course of time.

There are many things the Enneagram cannot do. Its power is limited. However, as a means toward self-reflection, spiritual practice, marriage, leadership, and evangelism, it is an incredibly valuable tool. Don't be fooled by either end of the spectrum—as a replacement for faith, or as an evil tool to be shunned. It is always at best a means to greater ends, a small light that helps us navigate our steps out of the dark, where we can once again be restored to the fullness of the true Light, Jesus of Nazareth.

The fruit of one's labors is always tethered to the love and impact of others. I would be remiss to not wholeheartedly thank those who have—knowingly and unknowingly—guided this project toward completion.

Thank you to those who have shaped me in my knowledge of the Enneagram. Most notably, thank you to Richard Rohr for beginning the journey in me. Thanks also to Suzanne Stabile and Ian Morgan Cron for their workshop in continued learning that was made available years ago. To my doctoral dissertation adviser, Keith Matthews, who guided my initial Enneagram project in 2016, I offer my sincere thanks, as well as to my friend Mark Scandrette, whose example inspired me to dare to teach the Enneagram for the purpose of discipleship.

Thank you to my spiritual family, Mars Hill Bible Church, for being a Jesus people for the sake of the world. I am grateful to be surrounded by many voices who proclaim the greatness of the Father, Son, and Holy Spirit.

Thank you to Katelyn Beaty for inviting me into this opportunity, and to Jonathan Merritt for guiding me along the way.

Finally, thank you to my wife, Elaina, and my daughter, Eloise. You inspire, encourage, and teach me so very much. What love we get to share together! Life with you both has, for me, redefined the meaning of flourishing.

Origins

Many Christians are suspicious (sometimes understandably so) about the origins of the Enneagram and whether it can be a trustworthy guide into authentic discipleship in the way of Jesus. Some believe it originated with Sufi mysticism, while others claim the desert fathers of early Christianity were the first to propose a theory of the human condition that evolved into what we now have in the Enneagram. Still others purport that it came from even earlier cultures. Although the Enneagram's origin remains somewhat mysterious, the path of its twentieth-century reemergence is clear.

Armenian spiritual teacher George Ivanovich Gurdjieff brought the contents of the Enneagram to the West, having learned versions of it from both Eastern Orthodox Christians and Sufis.[1] Some time later, Oscar Ichazo, founder of the Arica School, learned various forms of the Enneagram and combined them, it is believed, into the form that is commonly used today. About the modern Enneagram and its origins, Riso and Hudson say that it

> seems to be the result of Ichazo's brilliant synthesis of a number of related systems of thought about the nature and structure of human consciousness, brought together in the enigmatic Enneagram symbol. It is best described as a contemporary and evolving theory of human nature

based on a variety of time-honored sources and traditions. At the same time, it is quite clear that there is no single body of knowledge, no continuous "oral tradition" of the Enneagram handed down from antiquity. Rather, many traditions and innovations, both modern and ancient, have gone into the creation of this remarkable system.[2]

Ichazo eventually crossed paths with Claudio Naranjo, a Chilean-born psychiatrist, and together they brought the Enneagram to Berkeley, California, where Naranjo employed it through his practice. It was then proliferated through various Enneagram workshops, where, "in the early 1970s, several American Jesuit priests—most notably the Reverend Robert Ochs, SJ—learned the material from Claudio Naranjo. Ochs taught it to other Jesuits at Loyola University in Chicago, and from there it spread quickly."[3]

Opposition

Opposition to the Enneagram is rife, especially among Christians, because of its speculative origins, disputed psychology, and universal application. A significant example came in 2004, when the Committee on Doctrine of the US Conference of Catholic Bishops released a report questioning the credibility of the tool as a viable instrument of scientific psychology. The report concluded, "An examination of the origins of Enneagram teaching reveals that it does not have credibility as an instrument of scientific psychology and that the philosophical and religious ideas of its creators are out of keeping with basic elements of Christian faith on several points. Consequently, the attempt to adapt the Enneagram to Christianity as a tool for personal spiritual development shows little promise of providing substantial benefit to the Christian community."[4]

In a 2012 article in the *Catholic World Report*, reporter Anna Abbott claimed that the theory "encourages unhealthy self-absorption."[5] Certainly, as with any personality theory, this may be true in some cases, but one need not undermine all such theories simply because students or proponents of that theory abuse it. If that were the case, every personality theory should be dismissed. To the contrary, the Enneagram is designed to increase one's self-awareness toward transformation rather than self-absorption. In the same article, Abbott also suggests that the Enneagram encourages a relativizing of sin so that a person blames their type rather than taking personal responsibility. But this argument fails to consider each person's complicity in falling back into the default behaviors of their type. Far from relativizing sin, says Suzanne Zuercher, a Benedictine nun, the Enneagram "states in numerous ways that our greatest sinfulness comes from our desire to redeem ourselves."[6] Responsibility for sin thus falls squarely on the shoulders of each person, whose type serves not as an excuse for vice but as a resource for pursuing virtue and seeking transformation.

Mark Scandrette, a professor at Fuller Theological Seminary and author of several books, asserts that although the Enneagram has been scientifically validated, it needs no validation because it is "self-verifying through experience." He believes it should only be viewed as a tool for personal transformation so that we avoid using it maliciously to "shrink others down."[7] Much of the Christian criticism of the theory in recent years, Scandrette says, is due to its acceptance in New Age communities.

Another common objection to the Enneagram for Christian formation is that it "gives rise to a deterministic mindset at odds with Christian freedom."[8] To the contrary, the Enneagram helps identify areas of weakness, which, for the Christian, assists self-awareness for the purpose of greater transformation into the image of Christ through the Spirit's leading in spiritual practices and community. For the Christian it is particularly useful because it helps expose personal brokenness, sin, and shame, which can provide necessary clarity toward transformation. Sandra Maitri writes, "The Enneagram's deeper function is to point the way to who we are beyond the level of the personality, a dimension of ourselves that is infinitely more profound, more interesting, more rewarding, and more real."[9] Thinkers such as Maitri and Scandrette view the Enneagram through the lens of transformative *telos* rather than as an end in and of itself.

Still others protest the Enneagram as a new form of Gnosticism, pointing to biblical texts such as Deuteronomy 18:9–13 and the "detestable practices" enumerated there. The Enneagram, they assert, masquerades as a secret contact with divine energy and relationship with God that supersedes the need for faith in the death and resurrection of Jesus.[10] Father William Meninger of St. Benedict's Monastery in Snowmass, Colorado, conducts retreats on the Enneagram and centering prayer. He offers the following in response: "The Enneagram teaches self-knowledge. . . . Self-knowledge is the virtue of humility. Humility is the primary virtue. Self-knowledge is important to the spiritual journey. [The Enneagram] is only a tool."[11] Unlike first- and second-century Gnosticism, no promise of salvation is extended to those who understand or employ the theory.[12] Rather, one utilizes self-knowledge in order to pursue God (via the spiritual practices described throughout this book). The Enneagram is a useful tool for understanding one's motives more clearly and then moving toward transformation. It is a personality theory. And while it is true that some have twisted its contents into a form of religion, those who see the Enneagram as complicit with Gnosticism must see other personality theories such as Myers-Briggs and StrengthsFinder in the same way.

Finally, opponents must concede that earlier Christian communities drew on many core Enneagram themes, whether or not they meant to. Riso and Hudson affirm its Christian historicity: The "nine passions are based on the seven deadly sins, with two more passions bringing the total to nine. . . . The One's passion is Anger, the Two's is Pride, the Four's is Envy, the Five's is Avarice, the Seven's is Gluttony, the Eight's is Lust, and the Nine's is Sloth. To type Three, he assigned the passion of Deceit, and to type Six, that of Fear."[13] Even apart from decisive historical knowledge of the Enneagram's origins, much of its content is clearly rooted in the Christian theological narrative.

Triads

We all expend energy. To cease expending energy is to cease living. The Enneagram, connecting each type to one of three primary energy centers, shows us that we tend to expend energy in one of three ways. These ways of expending energy are also known as "intelligences," and because each cluster of intelligence centers includes three Enneagram types, these clusters are called "triads."

Figure 7

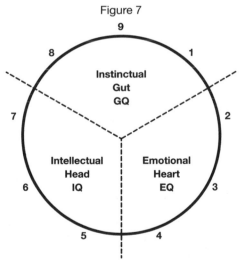

Types Eight, Nine, and One default to expending instinctual energy first. This is called "gut intelligence" (GQ). Types Two, Three, and Four default to expending emotional energy first. This is called "emotional intelligence" (EQ) and is symbolized by the heart. Types Five, Six, and Seven default to expending intellectual energy first. This is called "intellectual intelligence" and is symbolized by the head (IQ). The goal of energy centers is to notice what drives your decisions and how you make them. Once you identify your primary energy center, you can then seek to integrate the other energy centers in order to make wiser (and healthier) choices in life.

For Eights, Nines, and Ones, residing in the GQ triad means easily being able to read the mood of a room, trust initial impressions, and form quick opinions. They may be tempted to dismiss those in the IQ triad as inefficient and those in the EQ triad as caring too much about others' opinions. Twos, Threes, and Fours, who reside in the EQ triad, are feeling oriented and seek relational harmony. It is tempting for them to dismiss those in the GQ triad as judgmental and those in the IQ triad as insensitive. Fives, Sixes, and Sevens default to the IQ triad. They employ sound reasoning and rational systems in many facets of life. Increased knowledge, awareness, and planning helps them feel secure in life. It is tempting for this triad to view GQ types as too efficient and EQ types as dramatic. No matter the triad one defaults toward, the invitation is to surround yourself with others who can balance your intelligence and also to integrate the other intelligences into your own decision process.

As a presenting Three, I am an emotional person. Feelings matter deeply to me, and I seek to reconcile quickly if there is conflict in my life. This is often driven by my desire for people to like me. My wife, Elaina, reminds me often how dramatic I tend to be. She is usually right. She is a presenting Five, and I find her rather rational and cerebral. Far from our differences being a problem, our marriage is a blast because of the different ways we process life. The Enneagram has aided our ability to notice each other's default patterns. I tend to make the wisest decisions (at home, work, or otherwise) when I notice that my emotions alone are guiding my understanding and can integrate the other energy centers (intellectual and instinctual) for a fuller perspective. I make unwise decisions when I listen only to my emotions as a source of what is true in life. Because emotions are only one source of intelligence, I must be disciplined to integrate all of the intelligence centers (and invite others into the process who are different from me), lest poor decisions result. In the world of leadership, this is a case study for why plurality in leadership is helpful. In the realm of marriage, this is why mutual submission is essential for a thriving couple.

For a more thorough analysis of triads and how they work, see *Spiritual Rhythms for the Enneagram: A Handbook for Harmony and Transformation* by Adele and Doug Calhoun and Clare and Scott Loughrige.

Wings

The Enneagram is commonly referred to as the nine faces of the soul. But for some (particularly Sixes, who seldom find authorities trustworthy), the Enneagram appears confining, manipulative, and limited. After all, if all humans are only one of the nine types, why are not all Threes (or Sevens, or Fives) exactly alike?

This is where wings can play a vital role. Riso and Hudson write that "most people are a unique mixture of their basic type and one of the two types adjacent to it on the circumference of the Enneagram. One of the two types adjacent to your basic type is called your 'wing.'"[14] Further, Helen Palmer states, "No two people who belong to the same type are identical, although they share the same preoccupations and concerns."[15] Precisely due to this reality, it is imperative to treat spiritual formation as a diverse endeavor requiring many applications rather than a general approach to discipleship where unique people are given limited disciplines for formation. Even those who share the same type will experience variance in their personality that leads them to lean toward one direction or the other.

Wings can also be helpful when attempting to identify type because they provide a more nuanced picture of a person's tendencies and thus offer additional information to support the identification process. Riso and Hudson offer the following labels for each of the type-wing combinations:

1w2	The Advocate
1w9	The Idealist
2w1	The Servant
2w3	The Host/Hostess
3w2	The Star
3w4	The Professional
4w3	The Aristocrat
4w5	The Bohemian
5w4	The Iconoclast
5w6	The Problem Solver
6w5	The Defender
6w7	The Buddy
7w6	The Entertainer
7w8	The Realist
8w7	The Maverick
8w9	The Bear
9w1	The Dreamer
9w8	The Comfort Seeker[16]

Similar to ticks on a clock, some types extend further toward their wing than others. This is one way to account for personality

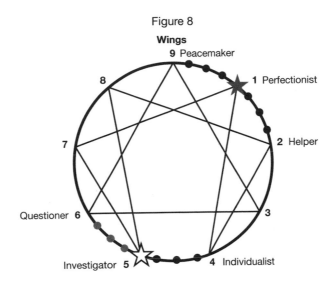

Figure 8

Wings

9 Peacemaker

8

1 Perfectionist

7

2 Helper

Questioner 6

3

Investigator 5

4 Individualist

variance within each type. Figure 8 shows a type Five with a Six wing, identified as such because of the person's tendency toward living with fearful anticipations. Proclivities such as this can provide valuable information in the assessment of one's type, especially given that some types share much in common. For example, it can be difficult to discern between Threes and Eights, Eights and (counterphobic) Sixes, Ones and Fives, and Nines and Twos. If the person represented in figure 8 is split between types One and Five, first understanding their wing can be key in eventually discerning their core personality. Riso and Hudson contend: "The wing is the 'second side' of your overall personality, and you must take it into consideration to understand yourself or someone else."[17] Additionally, a person may find that, in certain circumstances, the issues presented by her wing will be more significant than those of her type.[18] In other cases, however, the influence from the wing will be slight. Wings, to varying degrees, add to the uniqueness of personality type.

One of the frequently asked questions about wings has to do with whether a person can experience variance from one side of their type to the other, moving from one wing to the other. For example, using figure 8 to illustrate, since core personality type tends not to shift, is it possible to go from being 5w6 to being 5w4? Rohr attempts to answer this question through a lens he calls the first and second halves of life.[19] He suggests that for the first half of life, a person veers toward one wing, while for the second half one tends toward the other. These halves are not chronologically designated by years but rather by maturity. Therefore, one can and sometimes does shift from one wing to the other at a certain point in life, but without variance in their type.[20] Also bear in mind that both wings can influence a person's type, but at any given time, each of us will tend to be more dominant in one wing over the other, depending on what half of life we are in.[21]

For more in-depth analysis of wings, see Riso and Hudson's seminal work, *Personality Types: Using the Enneagram for Self-Discovery*; Richard Rohr and Andreas Ebert's *The Enneagram: A Christian Perspective*; and Beatrice Chestnut's *The Complete Enneagram: Twenty-Seven Paths to Greater Self-Knowledge*.

Practices

Historically, the Shema of Deuteronomy 6:4 is the most central Scripture in the Bible. Located in the Old Testament, it is repeatedly cited in the New Testament as Jesus substantiates its claim about who and how we are to love (Matt. 22:37–40; Mark 12:29–31; Luke 10:27). The Shema is a call to love God holistically (with mind, heart, soul, and strength) and to love our neighbor as ourselves. Therefore, Christian spirituality is a call to holistic formation. This is where spiritual practices come into play.

Practices (or disciplines) help us grow in neglected areas of our lives that remain immature and underdeveloped. Through the lens of triads (IQ, EQ, GQ), we can see how our faith is designed to shape each area of intelligence in our lives (head, heart, gut). The list of historic practices below is far from comprehensive, but it may be a helpful starting point. Each of these practices can be traced back to a long history of use in the Christian faith.

Head—Intellectual (IQ)

Liturgy

Fixed-hour prayer

Bible study

Scripture memory

Museums

Book study

Journaling

Heart—Emotional (EQ)

Centering

Examen

Lectio divina

Confession

Accountability

Sabbath

Inner healing

Gut—Instinctual (GQ)

Nature walk

Serving/missional engagement

Prayer walking

Labyrinth

Fasting and feasting

Hospitality

Silence

Mentoring

For further guidance in the area of practices, see Adele Ahlberg Calhoun, *Spiritual Disciplines Handbook: Practices That Transform Us*; Richard Foster, *Celebration of Discipline: The Path to Spiritual Growth*; AJ Sherrill, *Expansive: Stretching beyond Superficial Christianity*; and Dallas Willard, *The Spirit of the Disciplines: Understanding How God Changes Lives*.

Virtues

Every Enneagram type centers in a core virtue and a corresponding vice.

	Virtue	Vice
Type 1	Serenity	Anger
Type 2	Humility	Pride
Type 3	Truthfulness	Deceit
Type 4	Emotional balance	Envy
Type 5	Nonattachment	Greed
Type 6	Courage	Fear
Type 7	Sobriety	Gluttony
Type 8	Innocence	Lust
Type 9	Action	Apathy

This is not to say that each type has only one vice or that the core virtue is the only virtue one should seek. Rather, it is to help identify areas that are natural defaults and propensities and to begin to name specifically the kinds of people we want to become in order to imitate Christ.

Below is a list of virtues that have been handed down through the ages. These are not comprehensive by any stretch, but they provide the initial vision to begin the work of naming growth areas once you've secured your Enneagram type. I have found that considering practices that can help cultivate the desired virtue is most helpful. For example, as one who presents as a Three, I struggle with doing over being—in other words, it is easy for me to *do* (write, study, read, check email, etc.) and difficult for me to *be* (still, quiet, contemplative, listening). In order to cultivate the virtue of patience, I choose to begin my day with centering prayer.

Since we have discovered that all of the types are in you, feel free to roam the various virtues and identify which ones God is calling you to cultivate most deeply in this season. Note that this will change from season to season as you grow.

> **Pauline virtues:** Love, joy, peace, patience, kindness, goodness, faithfulness, gentleness, self-control
>
> **Cardinal virtues:** Prudence, fortitude, temperance, justice
>
> **Benedictine virtues:** Stability, hospitality, stewardship
>
> **Monastic virtues:** Poverty, purity, obedience
>
> **Augustinian virtues:** Faith, hope, charity

Foreword

1. Etty Hillesum, *Etty: The Letters and Diaries of Etty Hillesum, 1941–1943* (Grand Rapids: Eerdmans, 2002), 91.

Introduction

1. Don Richard Riso with Russ Hudson, *Personality Types: Using the Enneagram for Self-Discovery*, rev. ed. (Boston: Houghton Mifflin Harcourt, 1996), loc. 376 of 9385, Kindle.

2. Richard Rohr and Andreas Ebert, *The Enneagram: A Christian Perspective* (New York: Crossroad, 2001), xi.

Chapter 1: Identity

1. Henri J. M. Nouwen, "Being the Beloved" (sermon, 1993, https://youtu.be/v8U4V4aaNWk).

2. Philip D. Yancey, *What's So Amazing about Grace?* (Grand Rapids: Zondervan, 1997).

3. Henri J. M. Nouwen, *Home Tonight: Further Reflections on the Parable of the Prodigal Son* (New York: Doubleday, 2009), loc. 702 of 1977, Kindle.

4. Tony Merida, *Exalting Jesus in Ephesians*, Christ-Centered Exposition Commentary (Nashville: B&H, 2014), loc. 874 of 4549, Kindle.

5. Karl Barth, *Epistle to the Ephesians*, trans. Ross Wright, ed. R. David Nelson (Grand Rapids: Baker Academic, 2017), 89.

6. M. Robert Mulholland, *The Deeper Journey: The Spirituality of Discovering Your True Self* (Downers Grove, IL: IVP Books, 2016), 23.

Chapter 2: Personality

1. Karl Barth, *Epistle to the Ephesians*, trans. Ross Wright, ed. R. David Nelson (Grand Rapids: Baker Academic, 2017), 89.

2. Helen Palmer, *The Enneagram: Understanding Yourself and the Others in Your Life* (San Francisco: HarperCollins, 1991), 94.

3. Palmer, *Enneagram*, 94.

notes

159

4. Palmer, *Enneagram*, 72–73.

5. Palmer, *Enneagram*, 73.

6. Richard Rohr and Andreas Ebert, *The Enneagram: A Christian Perspective* (New York: Crossroad, 2001), 49.

7. Suzanne Stabile, "Know Your Number" (class lecture, Christ Church Greenwich, Greenwich, CT, March 21, 2015).

8. Stabile, "Know Your Number."

9. Don Richard Riso, *Discovering Your Personality Type: The New Enneagram Questionnaire* (Boston: Houghton Mifflin, 1995), 66.

10. Palmer, *Enneagram*, 101.

11. Palmer, *Enneagram*, 105.

12. Rohr and Ebert, *Enneagram*, 63.

13. Rohr and Ebert, *Enneagram*, 63.

14. Palmer, *Enneagram*, 102.

15. Palmer, *Enneagram*, 154.

16. Riso, *Discovering Your Personality Type*, 67.

17. Rohr and Ebert, *Enneagram*, 81.

18. Palmer, *Enneagram*, 135.

19. Rohr and Ebert, *Enneagram*, 82.

20. Rohr and Ebert, *Enneagram*, 89.

21. Palmer, *Enneagram*, 136.

22. Stabile, "Know Your Number."

23. Riso, *Discovering Your Personality Type*, 69.

24. Stabile, "Know Your Number."

25. Don Richard Riso with Russ Hudson, *Personality Types: Using the Enneagram for Self-Discovery*, rev. ed. (Boston: Houghton Mifflin Harcourt, 1996), loc. 2529–31 of 9385, Kindle.

26. Stabile, "Know Your Number."

27. Palmer, *Enneagram*, 168.

28. Palmer, *Enneagram*, 169.

29. Palmer, *Enneagram*, 170.

30. Stabile, "Know Your Number."

31. Riso, *Discovering Your Personality Type*, 69.

32. Rohr and Ebert, *Enneagram*, 98.

33. Stabile, "Know Your Number."

34. Rohr and Ebert, *Enneagram*, 98.

35. Rohr and Ebert, *Enneagram*, 99.

36. Riso, *Discovering Your Personality Type*, 70.

37. Palmer, *Enneagram*, 233.

38. Rohr and Ebert, *Enneagram*, 115.

39. Stabile, "Know Your Number."

40. Rohr and Ebert, *Enneagram*, 115.

41. Riso, *Discovering Your Personality Type*, 71.

42. Stabile, "Know Your Number."

43. Riso, *Discovering Your Personality Type*, 71.

44. Palmer, *Enneagram*, 205.

45. Palmer, *Enneagram*, 237.

46. Stabile, "Know Your Number."

47. Don Richard Riso and Russ Hudson, *Understanding the Enneagram: The Practical Guide to Personality Types*, rev. ed. (Boston: Houghton Mifflin Harcourt, 2000), loc. 4898 of 5577, Kindle.

48. Palmer, *Enneagram*, 238.

49. Palmer, *Enneagram*, 257.

50. Palmer, *Enneagram*, 260.

51. Palmer, *Enneagram*, 240.

52. Rohr and Ebert, *Enneagram*, 137.

53. Rohr and Ebert, *Enneagram*, 131.

54. Stabile, "Know Your Number."

55. Rohr and Ebert, *Enneagram*, 146.

56. Riso and Hudson, *Understanding the Enneagram*, loc. 4927 of 5577, Kindle.

57. Rohr and Ebert, *Enneagram*, 147.

58. Stabile, "Know Your Number."

59. Rohr and Ebert, *Enneagram*, 148.

60. Stabile, "Know Your Number."

61. Rohr and Ebert, *Enneagram*, 163.

62. Stabile, "Know Your Number."

63. Rohr and Ebert, *Enneagram*, 163.

64. Rohr and Ebert, *Enneagram*, 163.

65. Stabile, "Know Your Number."

66. Stabile, "Know Your Number."

67. Palmer, *Enneagram*, 345.

68. Rohr and Ebert, *Enneagram*, 178.

69. Palmer, *Enneagram*, 348.

70. Rohr and Ebert, *Enneagram*, 181.

71. Palmer, *Enneagram*, 348.

72. Stabile, "Know Your Number."

73. Stabile, "Know Your Number."

74. I recommend the Riso-Hudson Enneagram Type Indicator (RHETI), available from the Enneagram Institute, https://www.enneagraminstitute.com /rheti.

Chapter 3: Discipleship

1. Don Richard Riso and Russ Hudson, *Wisdom of the Enneagram* (Toronto: Bantam Books, 1999), 344.

2. Sandra Maitri, *The Spiritual Dimension of the Enneagram: Nine Faces of the Soul* (New York: Tarcher / Putnam, 2000), loc. 4753 of 5616, Kindle.

3. David Brooks, *The Road to Character* (New York: Random House, 2015), 263–64.

4. Don Richard Riso, *Enneagram Transformations: Releases and Affirmations for Healing Your Personality Type* (Boston: Houghton Mifflin Harcourt, 1993), 24.

5. Riso and Hudson, *Wisdom of the Enneagram*, 360.

6. Anthony M. Coniaris, *Philokalia: The Bible of Orthodox Spirituality* (Minneapolis: Light and Life, 1998), loc. 1098–99 of 9553, Kindle.

7. Adele A. Calhoun, *Spiritual Disciplines Handbook: Practices That Transform Us* (Downers Grove, IL: InterVarsity, 2005), loc. 224 of 261, Kindle.

Chapter 4: Scripture

1. Bill Woodrow, *Listening to History*, http://www.billwoodrow.com/dev/results.php?work_id=1987.

2. Ben Irwin, "Biblical Literacy Begins with Reading," Q: Ideas for the Common Good, accessed November 8, 2019, http://208.106.253.109/blog/biblical-literacy-begins-with-reading.aspx.

3. Carl Jung's work is especially helpful here.

4. Diane Tolomeo, Pearl Gervais, and Remi J. De Roo, *Biblical Characters and the Enneagram: Images of Transformation* (Victoria, BC: Newport Bay, 2002), 20.

5. Tolomeo, Gervais, De Roo, *Biblical Characters and the Enneagram*, 71.

6. Tolomeo, Gervais, De Roo, *Biblical Characters and the Enneagram*, 74.

7. Tolomeo, Gervais, De Roo, *Biblical Characters and the Enneagram*, 95.

8. Tolomeo, Gervais, De Roo, *Biblical Characters and the Enneagram*, 83.

9. Tolomeo, Gervais, De Roo, *Biblical Characters and the Enneagram*, 83.

10. John Barclay, *Paul and the Gift* (Grand Rapids: Eerdmans, 2015).

11. Tolomeo, Gervais, De Roo, *Biblical Characters and the Enneagram*, 173.

12. A. H. Almaas, *Facets of Unity: The Enneagram of Holy Ideas* (Berkeley: Diamond Book, 1998), 197.

13. Don Richard Riso and Russ Hudson, *Wisdom of the Enneagram* (Toronto: Bantam Books, 1999), 191.

14. Tolomeo, Gervais, De Roo, *Biblical Characters and the Enneagram*, 201.

15. Tolomeo, Gervais, De Roo, *Biblical Characters and the Enneagram*, 205.

16. Tolomeo, Gervais, De Roo, *Biblical Characters and the Enneagram*, 220.

17. Tolomeo, Gervais, De Roo, *Biblical Characters and the Enneagram*, 223.

18. Tolomeo, Gervais, De Roo, *Biblical Characters and the Enneagram*, 135.

19. Tolomeo, Gervais, De Roo, *Biblical Characters and the Enneagram*, 241.

20. Kathleen V. Hurley and Theodorre Donson, *Discover Your Soul Potential: Using the Enneagram to Awaken Spiritual Vitality* (Lakewood, CO: WindWalker, 2000), 75.

21. Tolomeo, Gervais, De Roo, *Biblical Characters and the Enneagram*, 96.

22. Tolomeo, Gervais, De Roo, *Biblical Characters and the Enneagram*, 99.

23. Tolomeo, Gervais, De Roo, *Biblical Characters and the Enneagram*, 96.

24. Tolomeo, Gervais, De Roo, *Biblical Characters and the Enneagram*, 127.

25. Tolomeo, Gervais, De Roo, *Biblical Characters and the Enneagram*, 130.

26. Tolomeo, Gervais, De Roo, *Biblical Characters and the Enneagram*, 134.

27. Tolomeo, Gervais, De Roo, *Biblical Characters and the Enneagram*, 138.

28. Tolomeo, Gervais, De Roo, *Biblical Characters and the Enneagram*, 154.

29. Tolomeo, Gervais, De Roo, *Biblical Characters and the Enneagram*, 164.

30. Riso and Hudson, *Wisdom of the Enneagram*, 74.

31. Tolomeo, Gervais, De Roo, *Biblical Characters and the Enneagram*, 171.

32. Tolomeo, Gervais, De Roo, *Biblical Characters and the Enneagram*, 244.

33. Robert Alter, *Genesis: Translation and Commentary* (New York: Norton, 1996), 53.

34. Tolomeo, Gervais, De Roo, *Biblical Characters and the Enneagram*, 253.

Chapter 5: Evangelism

1. A. H. Almaas, *Facets of Unity: The Enneagram of Holy Ideas* (Berkeley: Diamond Books, 1998), 44–45.

2. Sandra Maitri, *The Enneagram of Passions and Virtues: Finding the Way Home* (New York: Penguin, 2005), loc. 30 of 4722, Kindle.

3. Maitri, *Enneagram of Passions and Virtues*, loc. 30 of 4722, Kindle.

4. The Alpha course (https://alphausa.org) is a wonderful example of effective postmodern evangelism.

5. Frank Viola, *Insurgence: Reclaiming the Gospel of the Kingdom* (Grand Rapids: Baker Books, 2018).

6. Derek Webb, "Crooked Deep Down," *She Must and Shall Go Free*, INO Records, 2003.

7. Propaganda, "Crooked Ways," *Crooked*, Fair Trade Services, 2017.

8. Sandee LaMotte, "Bugs, Rodent Hair and Poop: How Much Is Legally Allowed in the Food You Eat Every Day?," CNN, October 4, 2019, https://www.cnn.com/2019/10/04/health/insect-rodent-filth-in-food-wellness/index.html.

Chapter 6: Character

1. N. T. Wright, "Why Christian Character Matters," in *All Things Hold Together in Christ: A Conversation on Faith, Science, and Virtue*, ed. James K. A. Smith and Michael Gulker (Grand Rapids: Baker Academic, 2018), 158.

2. Dallas Willard, *The Great Omission: Reclaiming Jesus's Essential Teachings on Discipleship* (New York: HarperOne, 2014), 80.

3. Wright, "Why Christian Character Matters," 157.

4. N. T. Wright, *After You Believe: Why Christian Character Matters* (New York: HarperCollins, 2012), 18.

Conclusion

1. For insights on leadership, see Beatrice Chestnut, *The 9 Types of Leadership: Mastering the Art of People in the Twenty-First Century Workplace* (New York: Post Hill, 2017).

Appendix

1. Don Richard Riso with Russ Hudson, *Personality Types: Using the Enneagram for Self-Discovery*, rev. ed. (Boston: Houghton Mifflin Harcourt, 1996), loc. 411–12 of 9385, Kindle.

2. Riso with Hudson, *Personality Types*, loc. 474–79 of 9385, Kindle.

3. Riso with Hudson, *Personality Types*, loc. 511–15 of 9385, Kindle.

4. "A Brief Report on the Origins of the Enneagram," US Bishops' Secretariat for Doctrine and Pastoral Practices, *National Catholic Reporter*, October 19, 2000, updated October 23, 2001, http://natcath.org/NCR_Online/documents/ennea2.htm.

5. Anna Abbott, "A Dangerous Practice," *Catholic World Report*, January 31, 2012, https://www.catholicworldreport.com/2012/01/31/a-dangerous-practice.

6. Abbott, "Dangerous Practice."

7. Mark Scandrette, conversation with author, August 5, 2015.

8. Mark Scandrette, conversation with author, August 5, 2015.

9. Sandra Maitri, *The Spiritual Dimension of the Enneagram: Nine Faces of the Soul* (New York: Penguin, 2000), loc. 3 of 5616, Kindle.

10. Maitri, *Spiritual Dimension of the Enneagram*.

11. Maitri, *Spiritual Dimension of the Enneagram*, loc. 137 of 5616, Kindle.

12. John Flader, "Enneagram Is Not Recommended," *Catholic Leader*, May 27, 2014, http://catholicleader.com.au/analysis/Enneagram-is-not-recommended.

13. Riso with Hudson, *Personality Types*, loc. 481–83 of 9385, Kindle.

14. Riso with Hudson, *Personality Types*, loc. 860–62 of 9385, Kindle.

15. Helen Palmer, *The Enneagram: Understanding Yourself and the Others in Your Life* (San Francisco: HarperCollins, 1991), 42.

16. Riso with Hudson, *Personality Types*, loc. 876 of 9385, Kindle.

17. Riso with Hudson, *Personality Types*, loc. 876 of 9385, Kindle.

18. Don Richard Riso, *Enneagram Transformations: Releases and Affirmations for Healing Your Personality Type* (Boston: Houghton Mifflin Harcourt, 1993), 37.

19. See Richard Rohr, *Falling Upward: A Spirituality for the Two Halves of Life* (San Francisco: Jossey Bass, 2013).

20. Richard Rohr, "The Wisdom Way: Scripture, Tradition and Experience" (lecture, Fuller Theological Seminary, Albuquerque, NM, April 25–May 5, 2013).

21. Riso with Hudson, *Personality Types*, loc. 869 of 9385, Kindle.

Almaas, A. H. *Facets of Unity: The Enneagram of Holy Ideas.* Berkeley: Diamond Books, 1998.

Alter, Robert. *Genesis: Translation and Commentary.* New York: Norton, 1996.

Barclay, John M. G. *Paul and the Gift.* Grand Rapids: Eerdmans, 2017.

Barth, Karl. *Epistle to the Ephesians.* Translated by Ross Wright. Edited by R. David Nelson. Grand Rapids: Baker Academic, 2017.

Brooks, David. *The Road to Character.* New York: Random House, 2015.

Calhoun, Adele Ahlberg. *Spiritual Disciplines Handbook: Practices That Transform Us.* Downers Grove, IL: InterVarsity, 2005.

Calhoun, Adele, Doug Calhoun, Clare Loughrige, and Scott Loughrige. *Spiritual Rhythms for the Enneagram: A Handbook for Harmony and Transformation.* Downers Grove, IL: InterVarsity, 2019.

Chestnut, Beatrice. *The Complete Enneagram: Twenty-Seven Paths to Greater Self-Knowledge.* Berkeley: She Writes Press, 2013.

Coniaris, Anthony M., trans. *Philokalia: The Bible of Orthodox Spirituality.* Lakeland, FL: Light & Life, 1998.

Foster, Richard. *Celebration of Discipline: The Path to Spiritual Growth.* Special anniversary ed. New York: HarperOne, 2018.

Hurley, Kathleen V., and Theodorre Donson. *Discover Your Soul Potential: Using the Enneagram to Awaken Spiritual Vitality.* Lakewood, CO: WindWalker, 2000.

bibliography

Maitri, Sandra. *The Enneagram of Passions and Virtues: Finding the Way Home*. New York: Tarcher / Penguin, 2005.

——. *The Spiritual Dimension of the Enneagram: Nine Faces of the Soul*. New York: Tarcher / Putnam, 2000.

Merida, Tony, David Platt, and Daniel L. Akin. *Exalting Jesus in Ephesians*. Christ-Centered Exposition Commentary. Nashville: B&H, 2014.

Merritt, Jonathan. *Learning to Speak God from Scratch: Why Sacred Words Are Vanishing—and How We Can Revive Them*. New York: Convergent, 2018.

Mulholland, M. Robert. *The Deeper Journey: The Spirituality of Discovering Your True Self*. Downers Grove, IL: IVP Books, 2016.

Nouwen, Henri J. M. *Home Tonight: Further Reflections on the Parable of the Prodigal Son*. New York: Doubleday, 2009.

Palmer, Helen. *The Enneagram: Understanding Yourself and the Others in Your Life*. San Francisco: HarperCollins, 1991.

Riso, Don Richard. *Discovering Your Personality Type: The New Enneagram Questionnaire*. Boston: Houghton Mifflin, 1995.

——. *Enneagram Transformations: Releases and Affirmations for Healing Your Personality Type*. Boston: Houghton Mifflin Harcourt, 1993.

Riso, Don Richard, with Russ Hudson. *Personality Types: Using the Enneagram for Self-Discovery*. Rev. ed. Boston: Houghton Mifflin Harcourt, 1996.

——. *Understanding the Enneagram: The Practical Guide to Personality Types*. Rev. ed. Boston: Houghton Mifflin Harcourt, 2000.

——. *Wisdom of the Enneagram*. Toronto: Bantam Books, 1999.

Rohr, Richard. *Eager to Love: The Alternative Way of Francis of Assisi*. Cincinnati: Franciscan Media, 2014.

Rohr, Richard, and Andreas Ebert. *The Enneagram: A Christian Perspective*. New York: Crossroad, 2001.

Sherrill, AJ. *Expansive: Stretching beyond Superficial Christianity*. N.p.: CreateSpace, 2017.

Tolomeo, Diane, Pearl Gervais, and Remi J. De Roo. *Biblical Characters and the Enneagram: Images of Transformation*. Victoria, BC: Newport Bay, 2002.

Willard, Dallas. *The Great Omission: Reclaiming Jesus's Essential Teachings on Discipleship*. New York: HarperOne, 2014.

———. *The Spirit of the Disciplines: Understanding How God Changes Lives.* New York: HarperOne, 1999.

Wright, N. T. *After You Believe: Why Christian Character Matters.* New York: HarperCollins, 2012.

———. "Why Christian Character Matters." In *All Things Hold Together in Christ: A Conversation on Faith, Science, and Virtue,* edited by James K. A. Smith and Michael Gulker, 157–88. Grand Rapids: Baker Academic, 2018.

AJ Sherrill has decades of pastoral ministry experience in places ranging from the beaches of Southern California to the streets of New York City. He currently resides in Grand Rapids, Michigan, where he lives with his wife and daughter while serving as lead pastor at Mars Hill Bible Church. Having earned two master's degrees in theology and a doctorate from Fuller Theological Seminary, he leads workshops around the world on the Enneagram, contemplative practice, and following Jesus.

about the author